Lucid Mind, Intrepid Spirit

Lucid Mind, Intrepid Spirit

Essays on the Thought of Chantal Delsol

Edited by Lauren K. Hall and Paul Seaton

LEXINGTON BOOKS
Lanham • Boulder • New York • Toronto • Plymouth, UK

Published by Lexington Books
A wholly owned subsidiary of The Rowman & Littlefield Publishing Group, Inc.
4501 Forbes Boulevard, Suite 200, Lanham, Maryland 20706
www.lexingtonbooks.com

Estover Road, Plymouth PL6 7PY, United Kingdom

British Library Cataloguing in Publication Information Available

Library of Congress Cataloging-in-Publication Data

Lucid mind, intrepid spirit : essays on the thought of Chantal Delsol / edited by Lauren K. Hall and
Paul Seaton.
p. cm.
Includes bibliographical references and index.
ISBN 978-0-7391-6768-7 (cloth : alk. paper) — ISBN 978-0-7391-6769-4 (ebook)
1. Delsol, Chantal, 1947—-Political and social views. 2. Political science—Philosophy. I. Hall,
Lauren K., 1980– II. Seaton, Paul, 1954–
JC261.D43L83 2012
320.092—dc23
2011044968

Printed in the United States of America

Contents

Preface

Paul Seaton

It is a pleasure to take up again the task of helping to make the thought of the contemporary French philosopher, Chantal Delsol, better known to American audiences.[1] This time I have an industrious co-editor, Lauren K. Hall, to share the work, as well as a group of fellow admirers of Delsol, incisive expositors and commentators all. This introduction is intended to provide the first-time reader of Delsol with a brief sketch of the woman, her oeuvre, and this volume. Afterward, her own words beckon, as well as a series of exemplary treatments of various aspects of her thought.

Born in 1947, daughter of a well-known biologist and conservative Catholic, Michel Delsol, chronologically Chantal Delsol is a member of "the generation of '68." Her intellectual independence from both right-wing Catholic thought and, especially, left-wing progressive thought indicates that this general category is far from comprehending all who came of age in that stormy time. She employs the distinctive French hybrid "liberal-conservative" to designate her own thought, but her conservatism is of a peculiar sort, as is her liberalism. For one thing, she prefers the modern notion of "the human condition" (made famous by Montaigne, later reprised by Hannah Arendt) to that of a fixed human nature, and she accepts the evolutionary character of the human species. For her, humanity is the "metamorphic species," constantly on the move, constantly changing shape. What remains the same, and what is to be conserved, become vexing questions. On the other hand, her liberalism's regard for human subjectivity is expressly indebted to Christian faith, it eschews Promethean endeavors of radical human emancipation and transformation, and is critical of most contemporary versions of liberalism. Like Tocqueville, she is a liberal, and a conservative, "of a strange sort." As someone who by means of the term "singularity" emphasizes the distinctively Western conception of the human person, she herself is a very singular thinker.

Moreover, she is, if not a singular, certainly a remarkable, woman. She early on married the center-right politician Charles Millon. They have five children and adopted a sixth, a Cambodian refugee from the Killing Fields. She has written about his harrowing life and the dramatic *rencontre* of highly civilized French life and the "wildness" of the far eastern orphan in *L'Enfant Nocture* (1993). She walks the walk, and not just talks the talk, when it comes to marriage, family, devotion, and sacrifice.

While raising her children she also pursued her studies. She studied with Julien Freund (1921–1993), philosopher, sociologist, student of Max Weber and Carl Schmitt, and *bête noire* of progressive intellectuals in France because he insisted upon the ineradicable antinomic character of human life. From him she received, along with the concept of the antinomies of existence, a model of intellectual intrepitude. She received her Doctor of Letters in 1982 at the age of 35.

Something of an intellectual late-arrival, since then she has been enormously prolific and enterprising, writing in a variety of genres, as well as establishing the Center of European Studies in 1993 (now the Hannah Arendt Institute) to foster collaboration and communication between Western and Central European thinkers after the collapse of the Soviet Union. A lifelong anti-communist, she early on came to admire the Central European dissidents, especially

Jan Patocka, and she has appropriated and expanded their thoughts on ideology, the human person, and the distinctiveness of Western culture. *La grande Europe?* (1994) and *Histoire des idées politiques de l'Europe centrale* (with Michel Maslowski) (1998) are two early fruits of this collaboration.

Her own contributions to "the question of Europe" are many and varied. Worth signaling are a book I particularly like, *L'Irrévérence, essai sur l'esprit européen* (1993) and *L'identité de l'Europe* (with Jean-François Mattéi) (2010), and a trilogy describing and analyzing post-communist Western Europe, *Le Souci contemporain* (1996), *Éloge de la singularité, essai sur la modernité tardive* (2000), and *La grande méprise, Justice internationale, gouvernement mondial, guerre juste . . .* (2004). Happily, the trilogy has been translated into English as *Icarus Fallen: The Search for Meaning in an Uncertain World* (2003); *The Unlearned Lessons of the Twentieth Century: An Essay on Late Modernity* (2006); and *Unjust Justice: The Tyranny of International Law* (2008).

Starting with its sheer volume, her oeuvre is quite impressive. To date she has written and edited or co-edited more than twenty-five books. They fall into various genres, including novels, studies in the history of ideas, philosophical essays, and cultural diagnosis. She is also a public intellectual, regularly writing for the daily press, including *Le Figaro*. There is also the occasional film criticism. All her work is intended to help contemporary Europeans understand themselves, their distinctive culture and history, their present, and their possible (likely, as well as preferable) futures.

Politically, she is a woman of the center-right, although in her own manner. She is a convinced Europeanist and an equally convinced federalist and proponent of subsidiarity. As a result, she has become critical of the character and trajectory of the European Union, declaring her opposition a few years ago to the proposed European Constitution because of its violation of these two principles. Likewise, she has tried to convince her fellow countrymen, especially in *La République, une question française* (2002), that allegiance to democracy and republicanism in France does not entail rigidly holding on to the current form of its social welfare state, state centralization, and elite, techno-bureaucratic, administration. Her critical voice is sharp, but always accompanied by positive counsel, and conveyed with a note of hope, one of the human attitudes she prizes the most.

The fact that she has won a number of academic and literary prizes in her native France (Prix de l'Académie de sciences morales et politiques [1993 and 2002]; Prix Mousquetaire [1996]; Prix de l'Académie française [2001]) indicates that her voice has not been without resonance. In 2007 she was elected to the Academy of Moral and Political Sciences, occupying the chair formerly held by the philosopher of religion and scholar of Islam, Roger Arnaldez.

France, therefore, has recognized her merits. For a number of reasons, we Americans would do well to take note of her as well. Coming to know her thought would expand our notion of "French intellectual"; it would add to our critical understanding of contemporary Europe; and it would help us to come to grips with our own version of liberal democracy, our own "late-modern" condition as an advanced democracy. At least since Tocqueville, France and America have served this sort of mutually illuminating role for one another. Herself a student and admirer of Tocqueville, Delsol would be quite pleased if this were to be the case for American readers of her work. I can report that this has been the case for those of us who contributed to this volume.

We begin in Part I with original translations of two chapters of Delsol's 2008 book, *Qu'est-ce que l'homme? Cours familier d'anthropologie* (*What Is Man? A Popular Course of Anthropology*). This is perhaps her most fundamental book, as it lays out her philosophical anthropology, the basis of human culture. In it she sketches the traits permanently defining the condition inhabited by humanity as it finds itself in the world. She also uses it to distinguish various cultural responses to this condition, occidental and oriental, as well as to shed critical light on contemporary Western societies. The opening and closing chapters of the book nicely limn this intellectual framework and agenda. Afterward, we turn to expositions of her thought.

I begin Part II with a *compte rendu* of *What Is Man?*, laying a foundation for the more specialized and targeted studies that follow. In general, they focus upon central aspects of contemporary democratic society and politics. Two—one by Carl Eric Scott, the other by Peter Lawler—deal with individuals in democratic society. Scott's essay concerns Delsol's portrait and analysis of what we have called, at least since Hobbes and Tocqueville, the modern individual, while Lawler's deals more positively with Delsol's own conception of the human person and his or her unique dignity. The political scientist and musicologist Scott makes good use of the polytropic David Bowie ("Changes") to illustrate Delsol's more abstract formulations, while Lawler characteristically emphasizes the unique historical and logical connection between our understanding of the personal character of human existence and Christianity's faith in a personal God. Lawler earlier made good use of Delsol's discussion of the value of care-giving during the deliberations of the President's Council on Bioethics (2001–2009) and he continues to highlight that theme in his essay.

From care-giving it is a short step to the family. Lauren K. Hall expertly develops Delsol's thinking on that essential "nest and nursery of our humanity" (the phrase is Leon Kass's).[2] Intriguingly, we learn of her observations concerning the recurrence of "matriarchy" in Western democracies. This is yet another instance when a wider perspective on things reveals progress to contain aspects of regress.

The essays collected here are far from exhausting their subject, but they present choice *morceaux*, in digestible portions, of the intellectual feast that awaits the reader of Chantal Delsol. After savoring and digesting the chapters in this volume, I counsel the whetted reader to buy the translated trilogy and take in her thought in its integral form. Then, I venture, some of you will have the desire to brush up on your French. *Bon appetit.*

NOTES

1. Chantal Delsol, *Unjust Justice: The Tyranny of International Law* (Wilmington, DE: ISI Books, 2008), translated, with an introduction, by Paul Seaton. Also, Editor's Introduction to an issue devoted to Delsol's thought, *Perspectives on Political Science*, Summer 2009, Vol. 38, No. 3, pp. 123–124, as well as an essay, "A Socratic on the Elysée: Chantal Delsol on 'The Clandestine Ideology of the Time,'" pp. 133–141. And finally, a review essay on Chantal Delsol, *Icarus Fallen: The Search for Meaning in an Uncertain World*, Society, Nov./Dec. 2005, Vol. 43, No. 1, pp. 92–97.

2. Leon Kass, *Towards a More Natural Science: Biology and Human Affairs* (New York: Free Press, 1985), "Is There a Medical Ethic? The Hippocratic Oath and the Sources of Ethical Medicine," p. 237.

Acknowledgements

The editors would like to acknowledge The Association for the Study of Free Institutions, The Golisano Foundation, the College of Liberal Arts at the Rochester Institute of Technology, and Dick Kaplan for their generous support of the conference held at RIT on Delsol's work, which formed the foundation for this volume.

We would also like to thank *Perspectives on Political Science* for their permission to reprint parts of essays originally published in a symposium on Delsol's work in 2009 and the Intercollegiate Studies Institute for their permission to reprint portions of Delsol's works published by ISI Books.

Part I

Translations of *Qu'est-ce que l'homme? Cours familier d'anthropologie (What Is Man? A Popular Course of Anthropology)*

Chapter One

Introduction to *Qu'est-ce que l'homme? Cours familier d'anthropologie* (What Is Man? A Popular Course of Anthropology)

Chantal Delsol

Anthropology is said to be a disappearing discipline. This is because its subject is disappearing. Not that mankind as a species is about to disappear from the earth, at least not in the foreseeable future. But in the sense in which human specificity, for all sorts of reasons, is losing its importance. Anthropology is a discourse (*logos*) about man (*anthropos*). For it to exist, man must exist but also we must want to say something about him. It is this last condition that is tending to disappear.

In this work, I will not take up the ontological question concerning man, which consists in asking what he fundamentally is. Whether, for example, he is nothing but a combination of matter, or (more agreeably, perhaps) a "waking dream," as the Chinese Zhuangzi said. One can ask the question, where did the first man come from? Was he created fully developed by a God who came to the sixth day of creation? Or did man emerge from a long transformation of animal species, one emerging from another? One can ask the question, in what does man consist? By dissecting a corpse, or even

3

cutting live flesh, one only finds matter, and never the vital human principle or some elusive soul. To such ontological questions are added the various beliefs (or doubts) about the intrinsic value of man, about the reality of his dignity.

I will not speak of any of that here. Here I am interested in what I call "the universal representation of man" found in all cultures, hence his existential "figure" or defining characteristics. Whether he is a combination of matter, a dream, or a fallen deity, it is the reality of his life on earth that matters. Here below one finds his identity as human, which one cannot take away from him, at least not without seriously wounding him.

This is the main argument of this book: I wish to maintain that an anthropological discourse, in the sense of a description of the universal human figure, is not "a chapter of imaginary literature" as Borges declared with respect to metaphysics. The human condition is describable, and it is not subject to our arbitrary caprices. In saying this, I do not base myself upon any particular metaphysics, on any ideological dogma, nor any religion. I address myself to all readers, no one has to have faith, only good will. It should be said at the outset, however, that each of the human traits I am going to speak about can only be exhibited indirectly by its converse, that is, by the indignation and the feeling of deprivation and misfortune that accompany its being effaced. In times like ours, when we lack all former religious, ideological, and metaphysical certainties, only the pain and suffering caused by its absence can indicate the reality of a trait. We can know that man possesses a given set of characteristics, a distinctive figure, because we do not accept seeing him disfigured.

CHARACTERISTICS OF THE ANTHROPOLOGY

One must distinguish philosophical anthropology from cultural anthropology. The first describes the characteristics of our species, the second describes the traits of man in this-or-that determinate culture. To be sure, it is very difficult to get the line just right concerning the distinction between the two. How can one know that a characteristic comes from culture or from the basic human soil?

Fortunately, we are far from the time when Montesquieu had to describe other peoples on the basis of vague reports or rumors. Today we have at our disposal numerous works of ethnology which make known the ways of life of most of the peoples on earth, both in time and in space. In addition, contemporary Western culture (perhaps especially since Max Weber) has acquired a remarkable self-knowledge that allows us to see not only what distinguishes us from others, but also what we share, what brings us together. Because of the latter knowledge we can say that the enterprise of philosophical anthropology does not necessarily belong to some utopian endeavor. Still, one must acknowledge from the outset its necessarily partial, and even biased, character. The author is so acutely aware of this that she was plagued by doubts concerning its possibility from the beginning to the end of her inquiry. The reader will judge its success.

Nonetheless, I do not intend to put forth an occidental cultural anthropology. Rather, I want to present a discourse concerning the human as such without bringing in cultural determinations, or prejudices. Some will say that such a discourse is impossible because all language is already cultural, and hence all thought belongs to some determinate cultural context that makes it necessarily particular. If this is the case, then no philosophical anthropology is possible. There would only be different cultural anthropologies.

But today the deep desire of many among us is to find traits that are common to all of humanity—behavioral, moral, and social traits—so that we can live by what unites us and not simply by what separates us. Convinced that it is the multiplicity of cultures that leads to hatred of "the other" and to wars, our contemporary is moved by a passion and desire for what is common to all, and wishes to put what it finds in high relief in order to replace barriers by bridges. In such a context, I believe it is possible to develop an anthropological discourse that it not simply subject to particularity and which concerns humanity as a whole.

To be sure, the legitimacy of such a discourses, whatever might be its content, depends upon a preliminary condition. For a discourse about man to be possible, the group "man" must exist as a reality (even if this reality is not radically other vis-à-vis other groups of higher animals, as we long believed in the West).

A philosophical anthropology is underwritten by the conviction that the human species is one, and that the profound differences of culture do not prevail over this unity. If humans formed several species, one could not seek a common condition for them. Their groups would require several names, and not a single one, "man." Historically speaking, one then could imagine that the primitive peoples were not (or are not) composed of human beings in the same way as us; one could believe that they were (or are) composed of not-yet fully developed human beings. In that case, anthropology as "discourse on being-human" would have no meaning.

It is true that the conceptions concerning the *specificity* of the human species vary according to cultures. For the three great monotheisms which form the Western core, mankind is an insulated species, separated from the animal kingdom by a unique bond with the Creator. Contemporary Western thought has preserved the belief in this insularity (even if it has abandoned its religious foundations) in order to protect the legitimacy of human rights. For the majority of oriental wisdoms, however, mankind is the most evolved living species but is not separated from the others, neither by man's dignity nor by his destiny. The various conceptions of the *unity* of the human species are also quite variable. A number of cultures see ontological distinctions in the midst of the species, which create (it is thought) several sub-species of different men. The distinctions among the castes in India and the distinction between male and female in Islamic culture suppose this type of sub-species.

These differences in cultural beliefs, however, do not rule out anthropological, that is, philosophical, reflection upon humanity as a whole. No culture denies that there exists an entity called "man" who everywhere exhibits similar characteristics and from one culture to another inhabits a thoroughly analogous condition. To be sure, the differences concerning the unity of the species (are its members divisible or not into sub-species?) and concerning the specificity of the species (it is far or near to the animal species?) will have repercussions when it comes to the form of the *humanism* that follows from or accompanies the anthropology. The West created a humanism of royalty (man is the lord of creation) and of equality (all human beings are human in the decisive sense). Other cultures birthed humanisms of sympathy (man loves all living things) and of solidarity. In whatever form, humanism is necessarily tied to anthropology because one must speak about man in order to articulate the norms of respect for him. One must know the human being that one respects. In this way, every cultural anthropology engenders a specific humanism.

HUMAN PERMANENCE

But by means of the ever-increasing sophistication of their technologies, contemporary Western societies have arrived at a point of constantly changing, even transforming, humanity as it has always been. In this situation, it is very difficult to know if we are in the

process (depending upon the case) of denaturing man or of amelio-
rating his condition. This, however, is not wholly new and unprecedented. As we will see, one of the basic characteristics of mankind
is his constant evolution and his capacity to transform himself.
Nonetheless, in view of contemporary metamorphoses some have
asked if a stable anthropology can exist, or if there can only be a
discourse on man that is provisional and probable.

Moreover, an important branch of modern thought denies the
very existence of anthropology, i.e., of any possible description of
man. Man in this way of thinking is nothing but a malleable creature, without any other distinctions than those he gives himself in
accordance with his changing desires and will.

In the face of these challenges, the aim of this work is to describe certain fundamental traits of human permanence and, at the
same time, to attempt to exhibit this permanence. This is possible
because we have seen in the recent past (and we have before us
today) many attempts to eradicate these fundamental traits, attempts which have not succeeded, attempts that have elicited revealing responses. Before them we have the inner certainty—which
needs neither further proof nor demonstration—that something
genuinely human was (or is) being profaned. What can no longer be
proved by dogma ("this is permanent because God willed it so")
can be evidenced by the horror we experience before its disappearance. To be blunt: societies (including contemporary societies)
which seek to stifle awareness of death, face-to-face solidarity, or
hope for permanence, reveal themselves, ever more clearly, as dehumanizing.

This human condition, however, can only be sketched in broad
strokes. This is because culture arrives immediately, orienting it in
its own way, by responding differently to the questions the human
condition poses to all men. To anticipate our results: the fundamental figures of the human are rooted—without exception—in a primary, predominant experience: man is always *elsewhere*. In be-

coming self-conscious he "exceeds" himself. He advances in the present dragging the past behind him and haunted by the idea of the future. He remains haunted, while alive, by the death that awaits him. While being himself, he seeks with an acute hunger the other. Knowing evil, he wants the good that escapes him. Rooted, he wants to be emancipated from his roots. Put another way, he seeks an inaccessible dwelling place through a succession of temporary way stations. These are the different faces of *elsewhere* that I have attempted to sketch in this work.

Chapter Two

Conclusion to *Qu'est-ce que l'homme? Cours familier d'anthropologie* (What Is Man? A Popular Course of Anthropology)

Chantal Delsol

Philosophy traditionally spoke of "human nature." According to Western Christian theology, man had a nature different, for example, from that of angels.

To say that man has a nature signified at the same time that he was a being of nature, that is, a determinate being.

However—still according to classical thought—contrary to other natural beings, man is free. This indicates that he is not solely a natural being. He can distance himself from nature, he even can contradict it. As a natural being, he is subject to the general and universal laws of this world. Being free, he becomes a singular being who transcends his nature. If he were simply inscribed in nature, he would not be free. One would therefore say that man does not have a nature in the sense Aristotle gave to *phusis*.

Attempts to liberate man from the determinations that defined (and confined) him in a nature constantly appear in the history of Christian-European civilization. This civilization describes man as a definable entity and not as a process of becoming, which is the Oriental way of thinking. And the understandable tendency is to want to escape from this confinement.

For about two centuries we in the West have witnessed a denial of the legitimacy of anthropology. Everything occurs as if we cannot nor should not say anything about man. This is a considerable rupture. This is the first time in history that such a refusal has taken root in minds. For the first time, man is described by an entire body of writing as an undefinable being, not because of his mysteriousness but because of his essential indetermination.

This history of this process-event is still to be written. Here, it is enough to say that it began with the ideologies of the transformation of man that followed the French Revolution. The goal of what became Leninism consists in liberating man from his condition—an immense and radically revolutionary project. The premises of this gigantic hope were already found in the West with Pelagius, who granted man the power to liberate himself from evil, thus escaping from his complex dual nature. The same is true of Pico della Mirandola, who connected human grandeur with what we paradoxically could call a multiple nature; because it contained all possibilities, it was indeterminate. Sartre was Mirandola's heir. With him, too, it was connected with an emancipatory hope, because the human condition, like an enclosure, weighed heavily on this suffering and internally divided being.

According to existentialism, man is best characterized by his indeterminism, i.e., by his ability to remake and fashion himself. He is "condemned to be free" (Sartre). While he never wholly escapes from the reign of nature, he becomes the demiurge of the nature he subjects.

With modernity, with the revolutionary epoch, and above all with Marxism and its successors, the nature of man became a moment in culture. Human nature was historicized, it was attached to time, it appeared at a point in the history of man. In this way it was relativized. Engels showed how essential human expressions (marriage, governing authority), far from belonging to an always given essence, appeared in history, transforming man. Now they can be modified in a reverse direction. The idea of human nature disappeared. This historicization represents a reprise, in a different mode, of the original Judeo-Christian myth of creation. The appearance of sin in the garden of Eden is replaced in Engels, as well as Rousseau, by the appearance of evil in history. In contrast, however, the original religious myth was held to explain the origin and foundation of a human nature that was unchangeable. The historicization of evil, on the other hand, exploded the very idea of an immutable nature.

The failure of these ideas and consequent efforts to realize them does not need to be demonstrated. No one has succeeded in liberating man from authority, from evil, from the difficulties inherent in having relations with others. From these unhappy experiences, though, there still remains the underlying illusion that man can be wholly transformed and an ongoing revolt against the "condition" which so many sacrifices did not succeed in overcoming. It resurfaces with a different visage, but with the same unchastened naïveté and obstinacy.

Nonetheless, historical experiences, especially those of totalitarianism, forbid us to believe that our will can recreate the human difference (*la spécificité humaine*), at least without disastrous consequences and human and social destruction.

But at the same time, the anthropological figure transmitted by the classical-Christian culture, which has reemerged after the failure of the ideologies of radical transformation, is subject to a number of justified critiques. It is a rigid, unchanging figure, which inscribes itself in a divine plan and rules out almost completely change. But recent scientific discoveries in biology, paleontology, primatology, and neuropsychiatry call this into question and assign man to *process*, by showing the continuity of the living both in time and in space. This rules out imagining the being called "man" as wholly fixed and immobile.

In this way, the modern anthropological critique of the classical view, which was the foundation of the radical revolutions, appears to remain valid even in the failure of the revolution.

We therefore find ourselves in-between, where the rejection of the classical anthropology seems justified, while no other, more justified, anthropology has replaced it. Hence, the preference for the void, or what is called deconstruction. Deconstruction often speaks in the register of disappointment and resentment. We have been unable to keep the promise of progress in the form of a fundamental transformation, one that would make us the envy of previous humanities. We learned to hate the past and the present for the sake of the future. But that future never came. Not being able to change the being that we are, we therefore have said farewell to it.

At the same time, the decline of transcendent religions, the relativization of the human by astrophysics, the newly discovered role of chemistry in the formation of everything that appears to be immaterial in man (his memory, his sentiments, his will), all this commits us to a vision of man that is very different from the classical anthropology. Man has become a simple product of nature, barely different from his ancestors, the higher animals. Claude Lévi-Strauss wrote that "the goal of the human sciences is not to constitute man but to dissolve him," i.e., "to reintegrate culture into nature and, finally, life into the system of physical-chemical conditions." For Michel Foucault, "man is an invention, and the archeology of our thought easily shows its recent date. And, perhaps, its imminent end." To be sure, this is not about the physical destruction of man himself, but about the figure of the human that anthropology had delineated. It is a matter of getting rid of his purported transcendence or his purported mystery. The aim is to reintegrate him into the material nature from which he never should have departed. Put another way, man will be a being who no longer has a distinctive face.

Despite the foregoing, the importance of reinvigorating anthropology is not immediately obvious. One can still imagine that man as we continue to conceive him today despite the revolutionary failures, that is, as an indefinite and hence infinitely malleable being, lends himself to all sorts of changes and therefore to a range of improvements. But the advocates of this view, including partisans of deconstruction, find themselves yielding to the primacy of the physical-chemical, as Lévi-Strauss's words cited above attest. They walk into the wolf-trap of modern thought. If man has no distinctive figure, he at least has that of a material being, and he ends by reducing himself to it. This roots him in not merely powerful, but immutable, determinations. But it is obvious that the bee of the hive or the ant of the hill obey biological determinations much more than man in the city. If man is entirely reintegrated into nature and is only comprehensible by science, he will rediscover a nature that is constant and certain. It will not be defined as it was previously by religion, but by science, which will deprive him even more of freedom. As a result, one cannot see how this wholly "materialized" human being would be able to claim the freedom to transform himself in a voluntaristic manner.

Thus, what we need is a representation of the human that no longer invokes a fixed nature, but a "condition" that one describes from human experience and which is confirmed by the evils that flow from the efforts to suppress it.

The human condition appeared at the moment when nature understood as a fixed essence was rejected. However, at the same time it was recognized that one cannot do without an anthropology. Modernity little by little replaced the word "nature" with the word "condition." Man no longer has an eternal nature, but his definition was rooted in history and was described vis-à-vis his situation. Not only his social, psychological, etc., situation, but his universal existential situation.

Rootedness in a culture yields a cultural anthropology: man is determined by the culture to which he belongs and he can escape from it only with great difficulty.

But rootedness in the human condition reveals a universal anthropology, one that is necessary, not contingent. One cannot speak of a condition except in view of what necessarily arrives: a destiny.

As modernity progressed, nature little by little became for us a condition. This nature had appeared in the West from an external factor, divine creation. Come from God, it had meaning only by means of the myth that rooted him in his relationship to transcendence, man understood as the image of God and free to deny Him. The human condition, however, consists in an ensemble of determinations bound to a distinctive situation in the world, a situation that is inevitable or unavoidable. Man must die; transmission of life and our humanity impose structuring filiations; and so on. Depictable thanks to the experience of centuries, the human condition expresses the mode of being of the being called "man" as it universally— *ubique et semper*—appears. The efforts to destroy it have, instead of freeing man, destroyed his very equilibrium.

While the nature of man was fixed (because determined from elsewhere), the human condition is moving, because it evolves along with man, and its precise determinations are always subject to debate.

Deconstruction as the denial of anthropology was an episode of the nihilism that served as a passage from the fixed to the moving. Man does not emerge from this passage indeterminate. Rather, his nature is transformed into a condition (even if this evolution was announced a long time ago).

The end of the thought of human nature signifies at the same time the end of the certitude I have called the lordship of man, where man by his absolute specificity was called to dominate the other living things by his intrinsic qualities. The lordship of man was included in the notion of his nature. But the concept of the human condition leaves open the question of this lordship, or more broadly, of man's insularity. It even renders it problematic, making it a matter of belief, not certainty.

On the other hand, one really cannot believe that the prerequisites of anthropology have been destroyed by late modernity, whether by its currents of thought or its scientific discoveries. Even if there are efforts to radically transform the human, e.g., to render him immortal, or to deny the distinction (and conflict) between good and evil, the limits of such efforts quickly reveal themselves. They end up ruining the very being they claim to liberate. It is in view of an awareness of these limits that one can, however cautiously, limn a philosophical anthropology.

As I have tried to show, there is a commonly acknowledged anthropological discourse, one found in time and in space. All the different cultures represent man as the animal who necessarily poses disquieting questions and who suffers by living these *aporiai*. All know that man is the being who knows that he is condemned to live in time. To be sure, in the East various "wisdoms" appeared that maintained that these questions are superfluous, illusory. While here in the West, religions considered them to be real and substantial, so much so that man was seen as being capable of taking upon himself their mysteries. Different humanisms came from these different visions.

In what concerns the status of man, the passage from nature to condition marked the appearance of a developing, metamorphic anthropology, tied to our human interpretation and not to dogma. It also was connected with a universal anthropology because it was founded upon experience found across both time and space. This movement and this universality connect the Western anthropology and the eastern visions of man. The question that is raised, then— an essential one because the philosophy of human rights depends wholly upon it—is that of the lordship of man.

Part II

Responses and Elaborations

Chapter Three

Between the Human Condition and Contemporary Societies

Chantal Delsol's Exemplary Mode of Being-in-the-World

Paul Seaton

Il y a aussi les esprit lucides, les amoureux de la vérité, qui traquent les conséquences des métamorphoses et cherchent honnêtement à quels dégâts cela nous mène: ceux qui se demandent à quel prix il faut payer le progress.[1]

Dans le domaine de la pensée, c'est le dogmatisme qui s'installe tout seul, et il faut une volonté vigilante pour maintenir la liberté de l'esprit, la primauté des questions sur les réponses.[2]

The seventeenth-century French thinker Blaise Pascal once said, I opened a book expecting to encounter an author and I found much more, I found a human being. This has been my good fortune a few times in my life. However, with Chantal Delsol I reversed the order. I first met her in person and was immediately charmed; then I started reading her books and my admiration increased exponentially. She has become one of my "short list" of contemporary interlocutors as I try to make sense of the world, especially that portion of it called Europe.

One impressive thing about her is that she is a very learned author, so she is constantly bringing to my attention fresh perspectives and intriguing facts and thoughts. Without her, for example, I probably would not have known some remarkable moral prescriptions in the Egyptian *Book of the Dead*, or about the Iks, a modern-day Ugandan tribe whose sad story illustrates the destruction of social morals and the moral sense. Nor would I have known about the frenzy of marriage and baby-making that swept Europe after AD 1033, when the anticipated Second Coming of Christ did not occur. All of these piquant details—and scores more—figure in incisive analyses of the human scene and are woven into thought-provoking narratives concerning the human adventure.

She also is a remarkably prolific author. She has written and edited or co-edited to date around twenty-five books, including five novels. In 2008 she published two books; I am going to provide a *compte rendu* of one.[3] It has a special place, in fact a fundamental one, in her oeuvre, so it merits special consideration. Let us turn right to it, starting superficially, that is, on the surface, with its title and subtitle.

I.

In French the book is entitled: *Qu'est-ce que l'homme? Cours familier d'anthropologie*. We rather literally, even woodenly, can translate as follows: What is man? A popular course of anthropology.[4] That is a start and we will polish it up as we go along.

The entire title contains two parts: it opens with a question, then it designates a "course" or path of inquiry into and through the subject matter. "What is man?" she asks. *Eh bien*, she says, I propose a popularly accessible course of study, one that is anthropological in the original etymological sense of the term: a *logos* or rational discourse about *anthropos*, about man (*l'homme*) or the human as such. Since not all anthropologies are created equal, she will have to distinguish hers from others'.

Hers is philosophical. It is a philosophic treatment, though, that can be popularly conducted and presented. In this initial presentation of her *modus cogitandi* lie many an important issue, including the questions: What exactly does she mean by philosophy? And, how popular can philosophy be and still retain its character as deep and comprehensive thinking? Due to space constraints I will be unable to say very much about these important matters, a fuller treatment will have to wait for another occasion. Because of its importance, though, I will point out this-or-that aspect of her concept of philosophy as we proceed. We can move things along at this point by raising a related question: What *motivates* her philosophical inquiry into man?

This question in turn divides into two parts. To answer it, one first of all has to ask what her understanding of the contemporary French and, more broadly, European scene is.[5] Her inquiry into man is a response to certain key features of the contemporary Franco-European world. The present moment is one that contains a host of challenges, they emanate from a variety of quarters, and they all need to be addressed thoughtfully and, she adds, hopefully (70). I will talk about them in a moment. Many, though, bear upon the meaning of being human. They converge upon "the question of man."

The inclusion of hope in her prescription points to the second question we need to consider. How does she relate to the contemporary situation as she understands it, what is her complex response to it? Her first or initial response is what we can call sentimental, if we have in mind the rich sense of the French term *sentiment* which almost always contains a cognitive component along with the feeling part. Certain features of contemporary life elicit "indignation" and even "horror" in her, as she senses our very humanity being "profaned" (15). As these terms indicate, she has a version of what some on this side of the Atlantic have called "the wisdom of repugnance." If Pascal was right to say that our hearts have reasons, she wants us to listen to our hearts. Some sentiments have cognitive value, they put us in touch with important truths, if initially in a negative or repulsive manner.

Looking a bit more closely at these two sentiments, one could note that indignation implies some notion of justice, of injustice being inflicted or perpetrated, and horror is keyed to profanation, i.e., to some notion of the sacred. Her reactive sentiments are therefore rather important, even essential, human sentiments, keyed as they are to objects of deep human concern. It would be well worth the trouble to track her subsequent discussions of justice and sacredness (as well as nobility and beauty, their *Gemini*) throughout *What Is Man?* Socrates certainly would be keen to do so. On the other hand, it is relevant to observe that *What Is Man?* is a philosophical anthropology, not a philosophical ethics, much less an aesthetics. One therefore would have to keep things in perspective: she most likely is not intent upon full developments of these grand themes here. However, Socrates would be right to observe that *where* a thinker locates justice and sacredness in the human condition is a telling decision on her part. Having read through her book, he also would note that she talks a good deal more about good and evil than the right or the noble or the sacred; nor is her notion of the good anything resembling what is found in the *Republic*, or in the *Nicomachean Ethics* for that matter. These, again, are telling facts, choices worth investigating.

This important investigation, however, will also have to be postponed for another time, in part because these topics are not strictly necessary for our expository purposes. Not all sentiments, of course, bear upon such apparently abstract objects as justice and the sacred. Some are more personal, that is, having individual persons for their object. This sort shows up in her emotional register as well. These include disdain and one of its expressions, sarcasm, and at another end of the register, something of a maternal affect. Both of these come out when she considers the plight of many disserved youth in France today and she is moved to denounce those adults responsible for it. The blighted lives of those who ought to be "new dawns" in society darken her mood, especially when those who contribute to the result are ideological hypocrites.[6] On the other hand, however, she swells with pride in recounting the courage of Muslim girls and young women resisting the violence perpetrated on them in the *banlieux*.

Whether her sentimental reactions be positive or negative, Delsol is always well in control of her emotions and herself (no hysteria here!). In keeping with, say, Aristotle's or Thomas's teaching, they are essential parts of the order of her soul. They are parts of the parcel which is her distinctive mode of being-in-the-world. Therefore it is more than interesting, it is philosophically instructive, to consider the various hues and movements of her heart during the course of her depictions and analyses of things. The philosopher's heart is itself a philosophical *topos*.

But these sentiments are not her only, they are not even her primary, mode of relating to the contemporary scene. If the heart has its reasons, so too does the head. In her case, many *raisons*. As we indicated above, she brings broad and deep learning to bear upon, as well as a rather self-conscious intellectual approach to, the scenes to which her emotions are keyed. In part she moves on from the emotional plane because some people lack them, and others deny the cognitive value of such sentiments. Some thinkers (Martha Nussbaum and Nancy Rosenblum are American examples) have declared that one person's shameful conduct may be another's self-and-life affirming pride and joy. So, Delsol needs to move to another plane.

As I have already indicated, in *What Is Man?* Delsol approaches things philosophically, in the mode of "philosophical anthropology" (12). This is something of a development from earlier perspectives she adopted. The earlier ones I would characterize as political philosophy and, to coin a phrase, spiritual sociology. For example, in a book entitled *La République, une question française*, she analyzed the French Republic and its commitment to certain notions of equality, liberty, and solidarity.[7] This was very much a work of political philosophy. As for "spiritual sociology," in a trilogy of books with the catchy English titles *Icarus Fallen, The Unlearned Lessons of the Twentieth Century,* and *Unjust Justice*, she analyzed "the spirit" (*l'esprit*)—the minds and hearts, hopes and fears, projects and rejections—of post-1989 Western Europeans, those trying to find their bearings in a post-communist world.[8]

In these three, she carefully described and analyzed a figure she called Icarus Fallen. He was also termed "contemporary modern man," the man of "late modernity."[9] Fallen Icarus formerly bore the excessive, false, and now quite dashed hopes of various twentieth century projects of Progress with a capital P. (Delsol instances Condorcet and Marx as earlier spokesmen for these sorts of hopes.) Deprived of them, he is now rather disoriented and struggles to come to terms both with his recent efforts and failures and the new world within which he finds himself. After the experience of the two totalitarianisms of the twentieth century, he has decided to thoroughly moralize the domestic order via an ideology of human rights, as well as the international scene via a distinctive conception of international justice and law.[10] Politics, with its deep pluralism of differing ideas of the social good and its constant potential for conflict and even war, must be subordinated to moral norms that guarantee peace, that enjoin respect, that are non-negotiable. So declares an Icarus with some new wind in his progressive wings.

Not without sympathy, Delsol carefully analyzed this post-Cold War European figure. As a philosopher, she did so rather comprehensively, *inter alia* in terms of his relationship to truth, to the good, to morality, to liberty and equality, to gender roles, to the past and future, and—especially in *Unjust Justice*—to the pluralistic realities of politics and culture. One cannot say, though, that the final depiction was flattering in either the objective or subjective sense of the term. She displayed contemporaries characterized by a deep hesitancy to confront patent realities and still subject to lingering, if reoriented, utopian intoxications. Having had his earlier ideological hopes dashed by a confrontation with the ugliest of political realities, that is, with communist ideocracy, and still experiencing social problems of all sorts that Progress was to have relegated to History's dustbin, he has drawn almost all the wrong lessons. Skeptical when he should have been a realist, dogmatic when he should have had a healthy uncertainty, he lives (to use Hegel's phrase) in a self-imposed inverted world.

During the course of her studies, she also, somewhat sketchily, related her contemporaries to what she termed "the antinomies of existence" such as the basic polarities of authority and liberty and need and scarcity, as well as the above mentioned ones of truth and falsity (or certainty and uncertainty) and good and evil. According to her, these constitutive polar structures of the human condition had only a "clandestine" or "black market" existence in the contemporary world because its occupants resolutely declined to acknowledge them; these constituents of the human world therefore could only appear in surreptitious or garbled form. This provocative set of images and claims was a harbinger of analyses to come. It was a way of introducing the fundamental category of her thought, *la condition humaine*, the human condition. In 2008, after several years of research and reflection, it was time to present her considered thoughts about it, about the core elements and aspects of being human (*l'être humain*), to the public.

II.

In *What Is Man?* she presupposes the earlier analyses of her con-temporaries. Now she cuts to the chase, she goes for the human center of things, contemporary man's self-understanding. She asks, what do her fellow Europeans think and say about human being or human existence (*l'existence humaine*), about what it means to be human?

Quite remarkably, she detects among her contemporaries a loss of any deep sense of "the specificity" or "the meaning" (*le sens*) of the human. To be sure, there is lots of talk about individual humans and groups of humans and of human equality and human rights and so forth, but underneath and accompanying it she notes an absence: her contemporaries are very wary of pronouncing deeply, much less definitively, about what it means to be human. Among other things, that risks being dogmatic and hence being judgmental or exclusionary. This reticence—often cast in a politically correct form—is quite telling of advanced democratic attitudes on the European scene.

This dearth of specific content-claims about "the human differ-ence" goes together, however, with a great desire to find some intellectually credible shared bases of human community and coop-eration. To cite her: "Today the ardent desire of many among us is to discern traits common to humanity as a whole —, so that we can live by what unites us and not by what separates us. . . . We want barriers to be replaced by bridges" (13).

It is this paradox and this challenge that sets her thinking in motion. To be sure, the brief reference to the contemporary eclipse of anthropological meaning—one she says is unique in human his-tory—needs to be developed. According to her, any significant proposition concerning what is specifically human today faces powerful threats. We can conveniently place them in three large categories. The dehumanizing challenges flow, first of all, from modern science, with its methodological presuppositions, its remarkable findings concerning human development and functioning, as well as the awesome powers its technologies put in human hands. Theoretically and practically, in a host of ways the modern natural sciences call human specificity into question. You might think of certain dogmatic versions of evolutionary theory or current debates over the moral status of the embryo as macro- and micro-level illustrations of what she has in mind.[11]

While she respects modern science and accepts many of its "recent discoveries" (189), she also argues that "science is not the only thing that [helps us] understand the world" (70). Truth be told, it is passing strange to observe many scientists—practitioners of a distinctive and quite noble human activity—denying in various ways human specificity (not to mention, as she does, human "transcendence" and "mystery"). There is something not-quite-right about that picture. As Eric Cohen has observed, "The achievements of science are among the noblest testimonials to the special dignity of man, the creature with wonder, the creature who refuses to lie impotent in the face of blind nature, the creature who seeks to understand the hidden workings of the world."[12] Socrates's charge against scientists of his day—that they lack self-knowledge, that their account of the world and of the human cannot account for themselves and their own wonder and curiosity, their passion for knowledge and their pride at knowing—continues, in too many cases, to be valid today.

The second broad quarter from which challenges come is, remarkably, the humanities. As the title of this set of intellectual disciplines would indicate, this is quite paradoxical because the humanities traditionally were seen as the storehouse of a wealth of texts and ideas about our humanity, about human greatness and misery, and about the human condition we all share. Today, though, for a variety of reasons they all-too-often are what another thinker, Roger Scruton, has entitled a "culture of repudiation."[13] In particular Delsol instances "deconstruction[ism]," whose very name indicates its "undoing" character.

She, on the other hand, illustrates the good use (*le bon usage*) of the humanities in her own conception and practice of philosophizing. In her capacious thinking she incorporates literature (both ancient and contemporary), mythology and history, political philosophy and modern anthropology, even a dose of Christian theology (albeit not in a dogmatic or confessional manner). I was particularly impressed by her use and analysis of myths (20–25), of the great "cosmological poems" (78ff.) from the ancient Middle East and Far East, as well as from Greece and India, to illumine structural features of the human world.[14] Of her it is true to say, "Let nothing human"—or from the humanities—"be alien to me."

Before we advance to the third quarter from which challenges to our humanity and to our human self-understanding emanate (contemporary democracy itself), we can pause, as she does, to consider some of the relations between the first two. She dialectically explores the relationship between modern science and deconstruction in the Conclusion of her book. Deconstruction—"the negation of anthropology" as she understands it—either banishes all substantial anthropological talk or it persists in maintaining man's "essential indetermination," thus in its own way following in Sartrean existentialism's wake. "Man" (the quotation marks are *de rigueur*) is a social construct, at bottom he is a plastic being, infinitely malleable—so goes the view. However, since this position is sooner or later belied by facts and shown to be rather incredible (the failures of the communist efforts at reengineering a new man dramatically brought the falsehood of this claim to light even for the meanest of intelligences), it then opts for the sole stability that the modern mind offers: modern science's various determinisms, grounded ultimately in "physico-chemical" laws of matter. The height of human self-creative freedom ends with the disappearance of human freedom, of human distinctiveness itself. This dehumanizing dialectical reversal indicates that the search for the truth about man must wind its way between them, recognizing that he in many ways is a "mixed creature" (*créature mélangée*),[15] hence a mysterious one.

Science and deconstruction are two sides (or versions) of what I just called "the modern mind." To these rather cerebral sources, Delsol adds developments in contemporary Western democracy itself, which contains a plethora of worrisome features and trends. These include Europe's well-known demographic crisis, its birth-dearth, as well as others connected with the basics of human existence—birth and death, coupling, parenting, and transmitting both life and a way of life to newcomers to the human estate. The current social welfare state in France, for example, is palpably unsustainable. Worse, though, according to Delsol it is dehumanizing, embodying as it does an unjust egalitarian notion of justice and manifesting the reign, simultaneously, of impersonal abstractions and degrading materialism.[16]

In many respects she follows the lead of her nineteenth century French predecessor, Alexis de Tocqueville, who detailed many troubling tendencies inherent in the nature of democratic society. For example, she writes of "the individualism of contemporary societies" and of the (only apparently) paradoxical coexistence of individualism and pantheism on the contemporary scene.[17] Both are well-known Tocquevillian themes. She, however, has more evidence—in both time and space—about democratic societies to go on than he did, as well as a distinctive perspective from which to consider contemporary democratic societies.

Thus, her basic response to these varied threats is to retort philosophically, to locate them within an analysis and portrait of what she, in the quintessentially French phrase, calls "the human condition," the "permanent and universal estate [*état*] of humanity." This is the "universal existential situation" within which humankind always finds itself, precisely as human. Once she does this, she can begin the illuminating exercise of comparing and contrasting the contemporary European scene with the human scene *simpliciter*. As we have indicated, she makes the case that many developments on the contemporary scene are, in the final analysis, attempted efforts to ignore, evade or deny the human condition. Altogether, she portrays a political continent or cultural region with many ominous clouds above it. To mix figures of speech: as a cultural meteorologist, she is something of a Cassandra. It is hard not to be deeply affected with cultural pessimism when one reads her book.

In the next section I will sketch her view of the human condition, in the light of which she detects such developments. But first I need to report another very important feature of the composite picture she draws in *What Is Man?* So far it has contained the human condition and contemporary societies. But in Delsol's view the two have been connected or mediated by other things that are quite important in their own right. In two words, they have been connected by culture and by history. Contemporary western societies are the latest incarnations of European culture or Western civilization; they occupy a distinct point or period within its historical development. As we saw, they are what she calls late modern societies, indicating that they are at the end of one period, modernity, which itself was preceded by other periods.

These are not merely chronological designations and demarcations, they have deep content and consequences. To give some idea of this, let me report two things she says about "the modern period" or "western modernity," they will give a sense of what she is talking about and how important these designations are. On the same page in chapter 1 ("Mortality and Differentiation") she writes: "The modern period attempt[ed] to free itself—to extricate itself—from monotheistic beliefs" (37); and "western modernity . . . wanted to totally liberate man from his bonds, his ties, his connections" [*liens*] (ibid.). The "modern" appeared in the West when biblical

religion was denied and when a concerted project of human emancipation from it and all sorts of other ties or obligations appeared.
Those of us in political philosophy who have studied the modern
philosophers from Machiavelli on are quite familiar with this sort
of characterization and claim. Scholars in other disciplines similarly talk about the dramatic shift in Europe from premodern organic
or holistic societies to modern individualistic ones, from feudal
pact (*foedus*) to bourgeois contract and consent. Delsol is far from
alone in this regard.

Nor is this attention to, and periodicization of, Western civilization her sole addition to the contemporary picture she draws. Delsol
learnedly goes back before the advent of the historical cultures or
civilizations to the dimly lit origins of humanity: with the help of
paleontologists she takes a look at Neanderthal man. In her view,
even though much remained to be developed and traversed by his
successors, with him humanity first appeared in the form of "self-
conscious mortality": the evidence for this is found in gravesites.
As another author (Hans Jonas) has written, there is an entire
"metaphysics of the grave" which the observant observer can un-
pack.[18] She is so intellectually intrigued by our great predecessor
that she talks about him twice, at the beginning (17–20) and near
the end (160–161) of her study of the human. With him "the great
enigma" of self-conscious mortality appeared, with him "man"
(*l'homme*)—as an individual, as a species—emerged as a "living
aporia." As a phenomenologist, she is keen to observe the appearance of distinctive, and basic or foundational, phenomena (74).[19]

There is yet one more important feature I need to report. She not
only goes back "behind" Western culture, she looks around it. That
is, she executes telling comparisons with other cultures and civilizations. For example, what one could call the core Western ways
of death and dying—in two words, Jesus' and Socrates'—are nicely illumined by the alternatives that Buddhism or Confucianism
provide. Her cultural studies both illumine deep commonalities

among all historical cultures, commonalities which point to and give access to a shared human condition, and they help delineate the West's *Sonderweg*, its distinctive path and character.

To summarize the totality of the picture she draws: Its foundation is the human condition, the estate that all human beings enter into when they are born, the "destiny" we assume when we enter the world and with which we must engage or grapple one way or another. In its soil she roots the various historical cultures and civilizations, with central attention given to Western culture. She limns Western culture's historical developments, culminating with a steady gaze on contemporary Western liberal democratic societies.

In venturing so far and wide, Delsol exhibits the boundless curiosity of the Western spirit, which started with Homer's Odysseus. She is a true daughter of the West. One cannot but admire such capaciousness, such sustained interest in the human as such wherever and whenever it appears. She also is very much a woman of her times, deeply rooted in them, deeply committed to improving her own *hic-et-nunc*. Given her understanding of the nature and imperatives of responsible philosophical thinking, there is much to consider, much to evaluate, and much to point out for reform in present-day circumstances.

III.

Now, putting on seven-league boots, I turn to her portrait of the human condition. I also will try to indicate its bearing upon the contemporary scene. As I indicated, it is quite illuminating, often critical. In my presentation, I will have to be unpardonably succinct concerning both topics; my apologies to Madame Delsol in advance.

Her depiction and analysis of the human condition is conveyed in six chapters, each a rather polished literary and analytic gem. Their titles indicate their topics, sometimes also her theses.

The first is entitled "Mortality and [Human] Differentiation." In it she argues that in a fundamental way "the human 'I'" or self and the awareness of "having to die" go together, they form an "indissoluble couple" (34). For her, the human individual emerges with self-conscious mortality, and historically, or rather: evolutionarily, the human species as such appeared when it infused death with the significance exhibited in burial sites and rites. The awareness of death inserts man in temporality in a new, deeper way. Denying him endless possibilities, it opens up new ones. Death thus casts more than shadows upon life.

Today, though, many contemporary individuals are turning a blind eye to the "great enigma" of death, which means that they turn a blind eye to a fundamental aspect of their very being. Paradoxically, though, they also seek in various ways to put death to death. All this however—this fleeing and this fighting death to the death—has adverse consequences for our lives and our humanity, starting with a loss of authentic human individuality, including a growing refusal to assume the burden of the transmission of life, and ending, perhaps, with a version of Jonathan Swift's miserably immortal characters in *Gulliver's Travels*, the Struldbrugs. The equilibrium of life is upset by inappropriate dealings with mortality and death.

At chapter's end, she recalls her contemporaries to the enigmatic reality of death by reinvoking the first clearly recognizable human, Neanderthal man. If he could confront it, can not—ought not—we? She then proposes that the two fundamental alternatives to the question the primordial man brought into the world are religious hope and philosophical resignation. Both admittedly make high demands upon those who aim to draw strength from, and live in accordance with, them. Even with that admission, though, she maintains that, for the sake of their very humanity, contemporary Westerners need to seriously reconsider the founding sources of European culture, Socratic rationalism and Christian faith, along with the founder of humanity as such.[20]

The second chapter continues the theme of mortality and argues that "A Society is [or aims to be] Immortal." In it she turns to two central ways that human beings seek to overcome their individual mortality, by individual "generation" or "procreation" and by "social reproduction," or societal and cultural "perpetuation." They both involve a recognition of "time's" great hold and destructive power over life, as well as of the means that time and being have granted to self-conscious life to continue itself. Both forms of persistence, though, entail a belief in something greater than one's particular biological existence, as well as a will for it to perdure. This belief and this will, however, are ebbing on the European scene. The current European demographic crisis hangs heavy over this chapter, but in her analysis Delsol goes to its moral and spiritual roots. In a way that reminded me of Pope Benedict XVI, she detects a pathological self-hatred widespread in European culture today.[21] The decline in the status of the nation as an estimable community of belonging and a recently revised and almost wholly negative view of European culture and history (now seen as a series of dogmatisms, imperialisms, and tyrannies) set modern individuals adrift and all but impel contemporary Europeans to narrowly self-regarding attitudes and behaviors.

At chapter's end, she states that if Europeans are to resume a vital participation in the historical adventure of humankind, they will have to assume new attitudes toward the risks and uncertainties of temporal existence. In a nice pun, she says that the future (*l'avenir*) belongs to the adventurous (*les aventuriers*) and the hopeful. As such, it belongs to those who practice religion (70) (although not necessarily of a dogmatic sort), rather than, say, technological rationality. In affirming the life-enhancing contribution of religion, Delsol could hardly be more countercultural on the contemporary European scene. She does have her allies, though, in men as disparate as Jürgen Habermas, Nicolas Sarkozy, and Marcello Pera, as well as the above-mentioned Benedict XVI.

Then in a third chapter she discusses ethics understood as a "universal[ly shared] intuition of good and evil," and hence of self-assumed "norms" of conduct guiding and limiting human freedom (71). This is followed by a chapter on "[Cultural] Transmission."

Man's moral adventure arguably starts when men add to their awareness of their common mortality an awareness of their freedom, of themselves as responsible agents who can inflict or forbear from inflicting suffering on their fellows. Norms to guide this choice necessarily surface, starting with the golden rule which is found at the origins of every human culture (72). Culture as such is a particular human grouping's shared and shaping answers to the enigmas that human being-in-the-world necessarily engenders, it includes specifications of good and evil, usually within some cosmological myth or vision.[22] In every culture, good is fundamentally what unites human beings, while evil is what separates. *Diabolos*—dis-joining—is the apt term and image of the latter (82, 87). Each culture, then, makes it own contributions to—refinements and specifications of—this fundamental insight.

The chapter on ethics is perhaps the deepest in the book. In it, she certainly says the most about man's inner life and our complex or "mixed" nature, as well as our deeply ambiguous relationship to the world, itself a mysterious compound of real and ideal, actual and virtual. Many modes of being and of human-being are at work in the moral act, in man's moral existence. To begin with, man is a creature of thought (*la pensée*; 71–72) and of "consciousness and conscience" (*la conscience*; 72); he is so in part, but only in part, because of neurological developments: there are mysteries to acknowledge here. As a result, he is "a being of representation" (ibid.): he can "double"—via images and ideas—himself, others, and the world. This allows for a variety of perspectives, a plurality of possible judgments, on himself and others. (While she does not say so, this may be part of the reason for human freedom, for liberty of choice. St. Thomas, for example, declared that *ratio est radix libertatis*, reason is the root of liberty.)

Nor is this heady capacity or content all that she discusses in this important chapter. Human regret and self-reproach, for example, are necessary components of our moral nature, as well as distinctive sorts of self-satisfaction. Aristotle was right to distinguish physical pleasures and pains from moral ones.[23] These specifically moral feelings presuppose consciousness and conscience and a set of distinctive objects. In general the objects are binding, albeit non-natural,[24] self-imposed "limits" articulating "the fundamental antimony of good and evil," or a recognized "hierarchy of moral values" (72, 80)—in short, "norms" or "normativity."

These are a distinctive human discovery and invention. The ambiguity of the latter phrase ("discovery and invention") reproduces Delsol's own. She is neither a strict objectivist about values, nor does she maintain that morality is a matter of merely subjective—individual or collective—valuation. She seeks to limn a middle position which is admittedly hard to discern, hard to articulate. The good is recognized and recognizable, but ever elusive; evil is easier to discern, but is always implicated in the good's Heraclitean nature of showing-and-hiding itself.[25] It is not surprising, therefore, that in the course of this chapter she acknowledges more than one mystery in connection with man's moral existence ("the mystery of the moral antinomy" [74]; of "the origin of evil" [97]; of human liberty itself [ibid.]). I do not think this is necessarily a defect in her thought. In any event, it is worth noting when a philosopher acknowledges mystery. More should do so, I believe.

The human condition also contains mystery's cousin, paradox. Paradox, I would venture, is one of the three or four guiding threads of her book. Mortality, for example, combines both "existential anguish" (38)—thoughts and tremors that go down to the bottom of our soul and our toes—and the more positive side that "all our ardor, our energy, our hope, in a word all that makes the salt and the sense of life, comes from the limits of time [each of us faces because of our mortality] . . . our actions take on a deep savour in their very ephemerality" (41–42). Self-conscious mortality also combines irreparable human solitude and deep human community. In Delsol's words: "All men know that they are mortal, this destiny unites them and at the same time separates them. They become 'individualities' in the midst of a common destiny, or if one prefers: in the midst of a condition" (20).

Culture and cultural transmission have their distinctive paradoxes. Man is naturally born for freedom, but the conditions requisite for him to enter into the genuinely human estate of being free entail all sorts of initial dependencies and prevenient determinations. Chief among them is the imposition of cultural norms on the developing human who naturally is unable to rationally consider, much less critique them. One does not choose one's native language. Similarly, culture fundamentally is the answers (*réponses*) a group and a tradition provide to the newest members of both, answers which are not selected and chosen by the recipients; they are given before the questions are raised, or can be raised.

The West, though, has tried to negotiate this conundrum by including as an essential component of its culture and its distinctive way of cultural transmission, the right and the instruments necessary for critique. Employing a phrase from the Czech polymath Comenius (1592–1670), Delsol maintains that the Western way of education traditionally was a way of "initiative, not initiation." It sought to equip its possessor for the adventure of self-education, not solely for admission into a socially defined role.

Unfortunately, contemporary French education, especially formal education, more and more refuses to transmit "contents" (105)—credible beliefs, specific moral and cultural values, and es-

timable models of living, *presented as such*—along with the spirit
and techniques of criticism. Appropriate skepticism has hardened
into dogmatic closedness, and real openness to truth's possibility is
mocked as naïve and castigated as implicitly tyrannical.

Delsol's thinking here bears comparison with Allan Bloom's
famous discussion of contemporary dogmatic "openness," although
she traces a somewhat different genealogy than he.[26] For example,
she focuses more upon the essential element of cultural transmission which is authority. The antiauthoritarian thought of the nineteenth century masters of suspicion (Marx, Nietzsche, Freud) was
uncritically imbibed and implemented by the antinomian "68ers"
(*les soixante-huitardes*).[27] Today's children are ill-served by con-
tent-less instruction which presupposes they already are autonomous human beings, capable of reasonable choices prior to the
various intellectual and moral disciplines imparted in the family
and the *école*.[28]

The penultimate chapter, while it deals with the warm topics of
love and friendship, is quite abstractly entitled "Relation & Distance." In it we get elements of what one might call an ontology of
human relations. Delsol first deals with the various *interpersonal*
ways—relations of love, of friendship, and of searching discourse—that human beings can partly overcome their "essential
insufficiency." Because of ineradicable aloneness (*solitude*) and
manifold need (*besoin*) human beings must enter into complementary relationships which, in order to be healthy, must continue to
recognize the human differences and even incommunicability at
work (and at play) in them. The tale of Narcissus expresses ancient
insight into this truth. As Delsol comments: "The true bond (*lien*)
does not run from same to same but from same to other" (156).

I was pleased to discover that this chapter practically opens with
Aristophanes's famous portrait of the circle men in Plato's *Symposium*. It (along with Genesis 2–3) is the locus classicus of human
erotics. The classical reference is a harbinger of things to come, as

the topics of love and friendship bring forth some of Delsol's most lyrical writing. She is obviously in love with love and friendship and while quite aware of their limits, illusions, and temptations, she is equally aware of their charms, solid satisfactions, and humanizing contributions. Her development of the metaphor of the bridge (*le pont*) to explore both relations of sentiment (love and friendship) and of truth-seeking discourse (philosophy) was, in my judgment, worthy of at least a minor literary prize (135f.). It reminded me of a central feature of Parisian life, the marvelous bridges across the Seine, and the engaging conversations I have had there, not to mention the charming lovers I have observed there. In reading it, *j'avais envie de me rendre au Pont Neuf.*

Unfortunately, however, the contemporary French scene also presents a number of troubling developments touching upon these central human desiderata. They centrally involve false notions of human *self-sufficiency* that take the heart out of *eros*. Walter Scott was right to speak of "the wretch, concentred all in self." Advanced modernity has concentred selves by declaring them already full, autonomous, and independent, and many modern individuals have internalized that message. They therefore believe that they do not have to look without for connection with those with whom to share the burdens of human incompleteness. Such sharing would be marked by the choice and risks of "fidelity," constant wonder (at the other), and that "giving of self" in which one, paradoxically, finds both the other and oneself. Thoroughly modern individuals are ill-equipped for such adventures.

The false notions of individual independence and autonomy also adversely inform the reigning notion of justice on the French scene, an egalitarian one informing the European welfare state more generally. Men and citizens are publicly deemed to be autonomous, that is, independent materially and morally (*latu senso*). When it is discovered that many are not, measures must be taken to empower them. This endeavor and its operative presuppositions are particularly visible in contemporary efforts to include the marginalized. Their shortfalls are addressed by impersonal bureaucracies, their various needs are cast as quanta, so as to be measurable. The person and his spiritual dignity are accordingly missed. So, too, is the self-respect that comes from working and earning one's bread, from contributing to social weal. The project of a "universal allocation" is the antithesis of the tough love—the demanding respect for personal dignity—that sometimes needs to characterize the state's dealings with its disadvantaged members. More deeply, it violates the "law of life" which is effort, work, risk, achievement—and failure.

In Delsol's view, a well-ordered society combines *don, dette, et due*—gift, debt, and what's due—in just proportions.[29] There has to be explicit room for the various forms of caregiving, of person-to-person gift and sacrifice beyond contract and entitlement, that all human beings need at the beginning and end of their lives, and many times in between.[30] Contemporary society, however, whose self-image is compounded of hyper-independent autonomous individuals and a redistributive state charged with the mission of realizing that autonomy, lacks essentials of human community (see 141ff.). In many ways it is becoming a "non-society," a dangerously dehumanizing one characterized by the ascendancy of abstract and anonymous pseudo-relationships rather than "the solidarity of the face-to-face."

In a final chapter she discusses the pair, "being-rooted-in" and "emancipation-from" (*l'enracinement* et *l'emancipation*), two constant poles of the human historical adventure. Because man is more and less aware of the manifold forms and sources of suffering in this world—especially injustice—he constantly strains against the limits of his given condition. Good forms of emancipation recognize currently ignored or even socially denied human "capacities" and they empower formerly marginalized human beings to become "masters of their own destiny" (165) within the human condition. Genuine emancipation builds "bridges to other [more human] *enracinements*" (172).

Unfortunately, Enlightenment thought earlier (165) and contemporary society today[31] have taken the human need and desire for constant efforts at emancipation to "immoderate" (170), "extreme" (167, 172), finally "perverse" (167, 171) lengths, with counterproductive, even "barbaric" consequences (169f.). In many ways she sees—as a famous phrase once put it—barbarians in Brooks Brothers suits in Europe (although the designer today may be Tom Ford). "Barbarians" because destroyers of human ties, present and past. It is deeply false to hold out the ideal of total human emancipation from all given or inherited determinations (174). True emancipation is the search (*la quête*)—often "perilous"—"for a [richer] rootedness" in society, culture, and the human condition (161), not an escaping from or radical transforming of it. That was the mistake of Icarus.

IV.

Delsol herself sums up the root of her depiction and analysis of the human condition as follows: "The fundamental figures of being human are rooted—without exceptions—in a predominant experience: man is always *elsewhere* (*ailleurs*). By becoming self-conscious he "exceeds" himself. He goes forward in the present dragging the past behind him, and bearing within himself the idea of the future. He remains haunted, while alive, by the death that awaits him. While being himself he seeks the other with a passionate desire. Knowing evil he desires the good that escapes him. Rooted, he wants to be freed from his roots. Put another way, he seeks an unattainable resting place (*sa demeure introuvable*) through a succession of temporary stopping places (*séjours de fortune*). These are the different faces of *elsewhere* that I have tried to depict here"

(15). One could say that in her own way she joins company with Pascal and Tocqueville in discerning the constitutive discontent and restlessness of humanity, aggravated by democratic circumstances. According to all three French thinkers we humans are gloriously grand and miserable, grand because of our self-conscious miserableness, glorious if we appropriately respond to our "excessive" nature, to the antinomies of existence that we, and we alone, experience.

Delsol's summary statement is precious, providing her own view of the key concept of her thinking about the human condition. Its significance increases when we come across her saying the following about her contemporaries: "[Nietzsche's] last man, largely representing *the western citizen of late modernity*, [believes/lives as though he] suffices unto himself, and he *seeks nothing elsewhere* (*ne cherche rien ailleurs*)" (68; italics added). These may be the harshest words she pronounces concerning her contemporaries. One can hope that it is pardonable hyperbole, intended with rhetorical purpose to jar her readers out of complacency. (This would not be the first time a philosopher has drawn her contemporary readers in colors and strokes designed to provoke and not simply describe. Rousseau was a past master at this, for example.) Even if hyperbolic, though, it helps us measure the depths of her concern about her contemporary fellows.

Delsol calls the human condition *in toto* "tragic"—not that she counsels or countenances despair or suicide! But we are born into and cannot escape a basic situation in which, as the poet Wordsworth said, our reach exceeds our grasp. In all sorts of ways Delsol wants us to see that the pleasures, joys and glories of our lives as human beings are inextricable from our *misères* (our miseries), starting with our self-conscious mortality. We can fashion our lives—especially in democratic circumstances—within greater or lesser limits but we are not self-creators, we are not autonomous "all the way down." We have to accept—gratefully and often patiently—at least as much as we reject or even rework. But, she quickly adds, rejections and reworking are essential parts of the human condition. Just not the whole. It is therefore hard to keep the human estate in view in just proportions.

Today, though, it is especially difficult. We too often oscillate between false images of ourselves as gods (independent, autonomous, self-creators) and false ones that reduce us to our animality or merely biological existence. Fortunately for her readers, Delsol is a very incisive guide to extreme misconceptions and projects, plus she offers a credible picture of human equilibrium. Whether she will be heard and heeded by her compatriots, of course, depends upon them. In this regard, she is more Christian than Cassandran, invoking hope rather than tragic resignation or despair. It is a constant uphill battle, though, and success is not guaranteed, and it will always only be partial.

These are quite sobering words, but exactly the sort that people dizzy with ideological fantasies and projects, or deeply deluded about the contours and limits of the human estate, most need to hear. She himself is one of the "lucid spirits" (see the first epigram) she praises during the course of her book who have cut through contemporary cant, she is a lover of truth (ibid.) who shows that philosophy still has life in it and that it still can powerfully and gracefully illumine the world and our place in it.

V.

As it happens, I found but one patently false word in the entirety of Delsol's book.[32] Remarkably, it occurred on the very last page. There she characterized her effort at grasping the human condition—"the essential determinations" of being human—as having been undertaken, or put forth, *timidement*, timidly or timorously. While one can appreciate her awareness of the magnitude of the task she set for herself, one has to demur from her self-characterization. One would have to look far and wide on the European intellectual scene to find someone more, or even as, intrepid as Chantal Delsol. This is yet another one of the lessons one can learn from her about thinking in sometimes scientistic and certainly hyperdemocratic times. She certainly possesses the "vigilant will" she herself says is required to preserve one's liberty of spirit in dogmatic times. This is yet another way we would do well to emulate her.

NOTES

1. "There are also lucid minds, those who love the truth, who track the consequences of metamorphoses [in society] and honestly seek [to discern] the damage they entail: those who ask: what price we have to pay for progress." *Qu'est-ce que l'homme? Cours familier d'anthropologie* (Paris: Les Éditions du Cerf, 2008), p. 17. Henceforth *What Is Man?* All translations from this text are mine.

The passage continues: "Progress worsens [things] at the same time that it improves [them]. As a novelty, it also brings novel corruptions, ones that no one had thought of. They are what a reasonable society can attempt to anticipate; what it, at least, can agree to recognize, and to call into question [once brought to its attention]."

2. "In the domain of thought, it is dogmatism that installs itself all by itself, and one needs a vigilant will in order to maintain freedom of mind, the primacy of questions over answers." *What Is Man?* p. 137.

3. Her most recent book is *L'âge du renoncement* (Paris: LES ÉDITIONS DU CERF, 2011).

4. The phrase and genre "Cours familier de . . . " was used by the nineteenth century French author, Alphonse de Lamartine (1790–1869). He wrote a famous *Cours familier de littérature* (1856). In 2001, another French philosopher, Pierre Manent, published a *Cours familier de philosophie politique* (Paris: Fayard, 2001), a magisterial survey and analysis of the contemporary political scene, with a particular focus upon Europe.

5. To comprehend her field of vision, one might imagine Delsol atop the Eiffel Tower. From there, in a series of concentric circles she first of all observes her native France, then Western Europe (including the Scandinavian countries), then Central Europe (especially Hungary, Poland, and the Czech Republic). America is somewhat eccentric to her vision, but she is far from unaware or uninterested in us.

It is probably necessary to inform the America reader, especially conservative ones, that there is not an anti-American bone in her body. She does expect her American readers to be somewhat familiar with the European scene, as well as to be able to make appropriate "translations" or adjustments of her analyses to the American scene. I, however, have found that all too often such expectations are far from being met. Hence the need for translators and "translations" such as me and this exposition.

One further note for the reader: Ever since the Cold War she has had an especial concern for Central European countries which were subject to Soviet hegemony. She was (and is) very much anti-communist, anti-totalitarian, and anti-ideological. She was especially interested in the witness and thought of the anti-communist dissidents such as Jan Patocka. Their articulation of the human vocation of "living in the truth" after the eclipse of "metaphysical certitudes" dovetailed nicely with her own sensibility and thinking. In 1993, shortly after the collapse of communism she published *L'Irrévérence, essai sur l'esprit européen* (Paris: Mame, 1993; Éd. de la Table ronde, coll. "Poche," 2005). In it, she attempted to find the cultural core common to the two halves of Europe, so as to help their reintegration. She is very much, in Nietzsche's famous phrase, a "good European." More recently, she published *L'identité de l'Europe* (Paris: Broché, 2010), sous la direction de Chantal Delsol et Jean-Francois Mattéi.

6. Americans are familiar with the type under the rubric of "limousine liberals."

7. *La République, une question française* (Paris: PUF, 2002).

8. Originally published in French, they were: *Le Souci contemporain* (Paris: Complexe, 1996; Éd. de la Table ronde, coll. "Poche," 2004); *Éloge de la singularité, essai sur la modernité tardive* (Paris: Éd. de la Table ronde, 2000; coll. "Poche", 2007); and *La Grande Méprise, essai sur la justice internationale* (Paris: Éd. de la Table ronde, 2002). In English translation: *Icarus Fallen: The Search for Meaning in an Uncertain World* (Wilmington, DE: ISI Books, 2003), trans. Robin Dick; *Unlearned Lessons of the Twentieth Century* (Wilmington, DE: ISI Books, 2006), trans. Robin Dick; and *Unjust Justice: Against the Tyranny of International Law* (Wilmington, DE: ISI Books, 2008), trans. Paul Seaton.

9. The phase "late modernity" invites comparison with its predecessor, late antiquity. Delsol does not fail to follow this line of analysis, of comparison and contrast between two transitional periods in European history. In fact she regularly contrasts the end-times of the Greek democratic city-states with developments in today's democracies, as well as the more standard late-Roman Empire contrast.

10. See my "A Socratic on the Elysée: Chantal Delsol on 'the clandestine ideology of the time,'" in *Perspectives on Political Science*, Fall 2009, Vol. 38, No. 4, pp. 1–9.

11. To address a possible misunderstanding: Delsol is not anti-science. She writes positively of "the recent scientific discoveries in biology, paleontology, in primatology, in neuro-psychology, [which rightly] assign man to process, by showing a continuum of the living, both in space and in time, and which prevents

one from adopting an understanding of the being called 'man' that is immutable and [singularly] specific" (189). She certainly believes that modern science levels justifiable critiques at premodern essentialist views of man (ibid.). She, however, has her reservations about its typical worldview and characteristic reductionisms (190).

12. Eric Cohen, *In the Shadow of Progress: Being Human in the Age of Technology* (New York/London: New Atlantis Books, 2008), p. 5.

13. Roger Scruton, *An Intelligent Person's Guide to Modern Culture* (South Bend, IN: St. Augustine's Press, 2000), and *Culture Counts: Faith and Feeling in a World Beseiged* (New York: Encounter Books, 2007).

14. Starting with the truth that man is a creature of "clay," that is, fragile, imperfect, mortal. See the section entitled "Les mythes et l'homme d'argile" (20ff.).

15. Page 92.

16. For a complementary treatment of the French social welfare state, see Dominique Schnapper, *Providential Democracy: An Essay on Modern Equality* (New Brunswick, NJ: Transaction Publishers, 2006), trans. John Taylor.

17. "One can find here [in the tendency toward pantheism] a contradiction with the individualism of modern societies. I believe that there is actually a coherence. The individual is too alone, too self-proclaimed, to be able to survive without some 'globality' which subsumes him. People claim or pretend he is independent, when no man can be; because he has lost his groups of belonging [*groupes d'appartenance*], he no longer has anything [to do] but to lose himself in a Whole. Put another way, western modernity, having wanted to entirely liberate man from his bonds/ties/connections [*liens*], impels him toward the temptation of self-disappearance" (37).

18. Hans Jonas, "Tool, Image, and Grave," in *Mortality and Morality: A Search for the Good after Auschwitz* (Evanston, IL: Northwestern University Press, 1996), edited by Lawrence Vogel, pp. 75–86.

19. "The mystery of the moral antinomy suggests to us [the need] to look for the site of its appearance, if it is true that a phenomenon can find elements of understanding [by considering] the revelations of its birth" (74).

20. Delsol, however, detects a growing tendency in the West to pantheisms of various sorts: deep ecology, a rise in Buddhism, etc. These attitudes, doctrines, and movements seek to solve the problem of human individuality and mortality by eradicating its subject, the self-conscious mortal. They thus undercut the Western achievement which is the recognition and valuing of the individual and, thanks to Christianity, of the person as such.

21. "Here we notice a self-hatred in the Western world that is strange and that can be considered pathological." "Europe: Its Spiritual Foundations Today and Tomorrow," in Joseph Ratzinger/Pope Benedict XVI, *Europe: Today and Tomorrow* (San Francisco: Ignatius Press, 2007), p. 33.

22. Culture likely is rooted in self-conscious mortality: "One can think that the intuition of the abysmal enigma [of death] represents the condition for the deployment of human culture. In order to go beyond the immobility of animal

societies, it was necessary that humans began to be aware that they are fugitive beings" (20). Culture transforms and "sublimates" (a key Delsolian term) biological instincts, by giving them distinctive human "meaning" (*un sens*) (48).

23. See *Nicomachean Ethics*, Book II.

24. That is, not posed by what she terms our biological nature.

25. I allude to Heracitus's famous dictum, "Nature loves to hide."

26. Allan Bloom, *The Closing of the American Mind* (New York: Simon & Schuster, 1987).

27. Marx critiqued the state as an oligarchic tool and façade; Nietzsche, objective truth and its various guardians and spokesmen; Freud, in a complex way, exposed paternal authority, including that of the Father. For the "68ers," see Daniel J. Mahoney, "1968 and the Meaning of Democracy," *Intercollegiate Review*, Fall 2008, Vol. 43, No. 2.

28. See Philippe Bénéton, *Equality by Default: An Essay on Modernity as Confinement* (Wilmington, DE: ISI Books, 2004), trans. Ralph C. Hancock.

29. In a more responsible way than most leftist intellectuals, or members of the Radical Orthodoxy theological movement, she employs the dichotomy of gift and interest (or contract) to illumine the one-sidedness of contemporary society. Her view is worth comparing to Benedict XVI's as expressed in *Caritas in veritate*.

30. One this theme, one can consult Alisdair MacIntyre, *Dependent Rational Animals: Why Human Beings Need the Virtues* (Chicago: Open Court, 2001).

31. "The western societies of late modernity . . . pursue the ideal of an emancipation without any limits. . . . This is a perverted emancipation . . . " (171).

32. There was one factual mistake as she was misled by an inaccurate translation of a line from Shakespeare's *Coriolanus* (27, #3).

Chapter Four

Delsol on Human Rights and Personal Dignity

Peter Lawler

Here's a commentary on a prominent theme found in Chantal Delsol's trilogy—*Icarus Fallen: The Search for Meaning in an Uncertain World, The Unlearned Lessons on the Twentieth Century: An Essay on Late Modernity,* and *Unjust Justice: Against the Tyranny of International Law* (all published in excellent translation by ISI Books).[1] Everything I say is based on something I learned from these three great books, but I've done some focusing, clarifying, and reconciling of her argument—not to mention adding to it here and there. So I'm not sure I've been entirely faithful to the letter or even the spirit of these books, and even the attempt to provide specific citations for everything I say would clog up my text without being all that illuminating. Almost every point I make, I will say, she's made more than once. My goal is to employ Delsol to make a distinctive contribution to understanding who we are.

Today's world is distinguished by its devotion to human rights. The idea that each and every human being has rights, according to Delsol, is an unavoidably ontological statement—a statement about what or, better, who particular human beings are. It is a statement about what dignifies each of us—our irreplaceable, immeasurable uniqueness. It depends upon human beings really being persons or

51

subjects or, as Delsol occasionally says, person/subjects. The future of human rights is intertwined with the future of our true understanding of dignity. We can't just decide to accord each other dignity; there's no stability and, in fact, no dignity in a merely social and readily changeable decision.

We acknowledge our true dignity through our true belief in our personal greatness. Rights only belong to beings who aren't anonymous, who have names, who are aware of and claim their undeniable exceptionality. The world, the rights claim must be, is full of billions and billions of exceptions to the impersonal laws that govern the rest of the natural or visible world. Those exceptions, the claim must also be, are far more mysterious and wonderful and lovable than the billions and billions of stars that the physicists claim to find so fascinating. The philosophy of rights must be based on the intrinsic dignity of the beings who mysteriously transcend the rest of nature. The idea of rights is incompatible with too much scientific skepticism about whether we're really different in any personally significant way from the other animals.

Our dignity must be rooted in what's most undeniably different about each of us—knowing about and being moved to thought and action by the precariousness and finitude of one's own being. Knowing that I die raises me above the rest of the animal world and separates me fundamentally from every other self-conscious mortal. An animal can be identified completely with his species. He can't die as a unique being, and he's unable to experience or make a claim for his uniqueness. Because I (the person) am open to the truth about *my* being, I can't truthfully live as merely part of some whole.

My point of distinction, my greatness, is, from a purely natural view, a wound. I can't share completely in the healthy contentment enjoyed by the other animals. I also can't help but be somewhat miserably dissatisfied with who I know I really am. Each of us makes a claim for dignity to the extent that we're proud of living well with our insecurity and uncertainty. Nothing great can come without noble risk or some dramatic moral adventure; that's why no other animal is capable of greatness. It's not easy for me to live well with what I really know.

I can't help but experience myself as merely a passenger in this world. I can't lose myself in some whole or cosmos or group, so I'm never fully at home. My truthful goal is to seek harmony—not identity—with the reality—including the persons—outside of myself. My search for a comprehensive and truthful reality outside myself—a certain standard of personal responsibility—is never completed, although I can't deny that I know enough to act or choose responsibly. As a dignified being, I can't lose myself in any reality outside myself; I can't help but live in some distance—both ironic and caring—from who and what I think I know.

My personal experience will always be, to some extent, one of maladjustment. I want to be good, but often do evil. The moral conflict between good and evil reaches through every person and is never fully resolved. I long for immortality—or to be much more secure and durable than my biological being allows me to be, but I know I'm bound to die. I have to admit that I don't really know whether I will continue to exist after my biological death. We self-conscious mortals can't help but want more than nature gives us, but each of us can't know for certain how and in what sense he gets more.

Nothing we know is great or dignified but the meaningful, moral adventures of particular persons. Nothing a dignified being does can completely reflect the unique and irreducible being he is. A person confident of his dignity always knows that there's more to him than he can ever display, and that he is somewhat obscure even to himself. That means he can't reduce what he knows and doesn't know to some doctrine or dogma. He also avoids dogma because he knows that his dignity doesn't depend on moral or intellectual impositions on others. His place is somewhere between the nihilistic extremes of relativism and fanaticism. A man confident of his dignity doesn't feign indifference to the questions he can't help but ask, but neither does he aggressively assert to be true what he knows to be, at best, uncertain or partially true.

The person/subject pursues personal perfection. All human perfection—and finally all human meaning—is personal, not collective. When the person identifies himself entirely with some group or collectivity it's always by seeing himself as less than he really is. Delsol, for that reason, is hard on every conceivable form of identity politics. Nobody is merely black or white, man or woman, hetero- or homosexual, Christian or Jew, citizen or alien, husband or daughter, or member of some species. Destiny is always personal, not collective. "The good" always applies to and is found in real human beings. It is never conceptual, abstract or impersonal: Only particular flesh-and-blood human beings are lovable. The mysterious, irreducible, irreplaceable uniqueness of human beings is the source of both dignity and love, and there's no adequate conception of justice or rights that abstracts from either dignity or love.

Our finitude and precariousness at the foundation of both dignity and love can also make us repulsive to ourselves. So a perennial personal temptation is to care more for theological or theoretical visions of human perfection than who we actually are. It's tough—but, according to Delsol, what's most properly and uniquely human—to care for what and especially who really exists. We dignified beings are much more caregivers than producers. Our products or inventions aren't lovable and dignified at all, and that goes, of course, for our abstract or idealistic and always reductionistic distortions of who we are. Loving, solicitous, generous caregiving corresponds to the immeasurable, irreplaceable beings each of us is better than production—which is about measurable, standardized, anonymous results.

Caregiving and production are indispensable and incommensurable human activities; we can't do without either. But the one that attends more to invisible mystery and less to visible display is actually more dignified. Caregiving is not only directed to particular persons, but to our cultural and institutional inheritances on which every finite human subject depends for the shaping of his personhood. Only abstract beings—reductionistic products of our imaginations—can exist outside a particular, problematic cultural context in the pure domain of unmediated truth. Unquestionable certainty—or the wholesale replacement of "convention" by "nature"—is never a characteristic of a particular human being or a particular culture, and the interdependence of personal dignity and cultural inheritance is an inevitable mark of the finitude of both.

THE PERSON AS A MODERN INVENTION

The person/subject, Delsol seems to claim, didn't always exist. He is both the creation and the point of the modern world. In the past, men spoke of honor, but now they speak of dignity. In both cases, they mean to speak of their greatness. Honor was achieved through an exhausting effort to live up to some externally defined standard—the reigning code of honor. Honor had to be earned, and it wasn't up to the particular human being to decide what honor was or what to do to earn it. In those days, men thought they knew how to live, what they were supposed to do. The premodern world was composed of "holistic" or organic societies, where a man found his meaning by finding his place in a whole outside himself. He knew his place, and so he felt the maladjustment or alienation that's characteristic of the being open to the truth much less than we do. In the premodern world, meaning was imposed on particular people, and so personal opinion, strictly speaking, was unimaginable. The unity that formed opinion was not the person, and the person found purposeful opinions as part of that greater unity.

The Christians, strictly speaking, discovered the person. The Christian could, from the beginning, differentiate himself from all impersonal or collective wholes with a belief in a personal conscience, a personal immortality, and a personal relationship with God. The premodern Christian, however, still understood himself to work out his unique destiny in a communitarian context and with numerous cultural certitudes. He didn't doubt what came after death or achieve any distance from what he believed to be the true source of cultural authority.

Modern European culture is distinguished by the conscious intention to make the personal insight of the Christians more consistent and real. The modern invention of the person or subject was based, Delsol contends, on the ambitious intuition that each human being could flourish as a coherent entity. That meant that particular persons were to be far more completely liberated from the virtual cloning of selves characteristic of holistic societies for real personal responsibility. He would much more consciously and consistently come to terms with what he can't help know about his personal contingency and mortality. He self-understanding would become less anonymous; he would see himself more clearly as a unique, irreplaceable being with a name.

Personal dignity is most clearly displayed, Desol says, only in societies where the subject comes first. The modern subject seems somehow both a novel invention and a more truthful reflection of what beings like ourselves have always known, quite imperfectly, about ourselves. Personal dignity is based on a true ontological intuition about who we are. Acting on an ontological intuition is not self-creation. Delsol's opinion is clearly not that human ontology is a tale of man making himself over time.

When we live in light of the truth, it seems, we see ourselves as persons, and we discover our dignity. But human beings haven't always or even usually done that, and so they were somewhat blind to what they had the capability to know. Honor, we know, was a distorted but somewhat plausible view of dignity, and so even when honorable men didn't understand themselves correctly—as persons—they still displayed much of the greatness of who they are. Delsol shows us in various ways that her presentation of premodern man as merely a part of some collectivity is an exaggeration. She also seems to say, however, that only the modern person or subject fully sees his own dignity for what it is.

The modern intention was that each man become more dignified. He would assume the responsibility of a person, which is not freedom from being human, from our precariousness and finiteness. The thought was that we would become more aware than ever of our personal limits, and each of us would display the dignity of facing up to them. Modern liberation was not meant to be the pursuit of an illusory emotional and intellectual freedom from other people. It was for a more conscious coming to terms with finiteness through a more deliberate involving of oneself in the world. That involvement would be based our limited but real ability to share moral truths in common and to love and care for each other and the world we share.

The modern person would even affirm his need for some limited identification with specific places and institutions. The person can't dispense with being a citizen, a parent, and a devoted participant in various local communities. He doesn't aim to detach himself wholly from his territorial roots. Delsol says the person is aware of his incarnation, and so his beneficial dependence on various institutional forms of embodiment. He certainly doesn't want to detach himself from the conditions that allow us to know and love particular persons. The truth is we can't exist without all kinds of determinations, and so the person situates himself in a precarious position between under- and over-determination. He doesn't lose his personal identity in any external whole. while understanding his identity as personal, not abstract or disembodied. The place here between abstract universalism and unself-conscious communitarian-ism is as precarious, it seems, as personal existence itself. Because there's no single, certain, or perfect, way of finding that place, efforts to achieve it in freedom are the highest cause of the diversity that characterizes cultural and political life.

DISSIDENT RESPONSIBILITY

Delsol sometimes suggests that the modern intention was that every human being live a heroic life of personal responsibility. She sometimes takes her bearings from those extraordinary dissidents (such as the Czech Jan Patocka) who displayed their dignity in neon letters by living in courageous resistance to communist totalitarianism. The dignified person is always resisting, it seems, the dominant forms of depersonalization—the various forms of flight from the truth—in his time. The dissident's resistance to the depersonalizing lie of ideology was illuminated, Delsol says, by a source of meaning outside of himself, but he never forgot that his comprehension of that source was incomplete and uncertain. Patocka called that life of a searcher "negative Platonism," a refusal ever to replace the dialectical pursuit with dogma.[2] Patocka's amazing courage—his giving of his life—was in the service of saving the subject—the being responsible and animated enough to engage in meaningful search—from being absorbed in an impersonal, ideological lie. The dissident didn't act blindly or absurdly; his dignity was evident enough to himself to be able to act with truthful responsibility.

The fall of communism may have reminded us of the limits of the dissidents and Delsol's sometimes high idea of personal dignity or greatness. The experience of heroically resisting depersonalization has not yet been routinized or become the foundation for most ordinary lives. It hasn't become the foundation of the various post-communist regimes in Europe. How could most people ordinarily be dissidents? In *Democracy in America*, Alexis de Tocqueville thought that Americans could preserve their political liberty only because they quite consciously subordinated themselves to religious dogma. Living well in freedom seems to depend on affirming answers to certain fundamental questions without discussion. Some reliance on dogma, according to Tocqueville, is in accord with the truth about our precarious and limited condition.[3] The view of American students of Leo Strauss—who often think of themselves as negative or zetetic Platonists—is similar; the Socratic way of life can't be for most people most of the time.[4]

Most people most of the time, Platonists think, can't live well in light of the truth and nothing but. They need to limit their doubt and affirm some cultural certitudes with their hearts and minds in order to find what personal integrity they can. Patocka, I have to add, might have been extreme among the dissidents in his identification of meaning with uncertainty. Aleksandr Solzhenitsyn and Vaclav Havel, for example, seem more certain that there is a clear ontological foundation—a foundation in a reality higher and greater than ourselves—for dignified, personal responsibility. Havel and Solzhenitsyn were often less than clear about what or who that higher reality is, and to what or to whom the person is conscientiously responsible. But they seemed to have no doubt about the reality of a dignified, personal "I" who can and should resist absorption into the anonymous crowd.[5]

The American philosopher/novelist Walker Percy provides a defense of the view that the person is always, to some extent, a dissident. We can say that the being who wonders seems to necessarily wander. He can't really locate himself completely in the natural world that scientists can truthfully describe. Nor can he locate himself securely in the political community or "cave" that the best citizens can fully describe. The wandering personal dissident is in constant, caring search for loving harmony, but not identity, with other persons, including, perhaps, the personal God. The being who knows he wonders and wanders can't help but know that the only beings deeply worthy of his wonder, his care, and his love are other persons.[6] Human searchers can care truthfully for the culture they inhabit without being certain of the truth of any cultural or even personal answer to any fundamental human questions. Maybe it's still the case, however, that the dissident or, we might say, the person who fully displays his dignity, must be the exception to the rule among human beings. The anti-communist dissidents, we remember, also dissented from the banality of ordinary life in the West, and even Tocqueville knew he was too hard on the comparatively unmemorable way most people live.[7]

Delsol actually shows us that all the evidence we have so far is that the personal responsibility required of the modern subject has been too hard. That's why she goes as far as to say that the modern subject or person, strictly speaking, has not yet been born. We still can't say that the person or subject can even be a realistic model of human excellence for guiding a particular culture or society. Most modern men have fallen prey to depersonalization, to thinking and experiencing themselves as less than who they really are. The two forms of modern society of the twentieth century—ideological totalitarianism and the individualism prevalent today—have not even had the intention of forming persons or subjects ready to think and act for themselves.

THE MODERN INDIVIDUAL

Men today mourn the fact that they both seem to lack what it takes to become subjects and are stuck with an equally impotent and very selectively nostalgic longing to regress to organic society. Their real complaint is that they're stuck in a place where it's so hard to know who they are or what to do. They're especially displaced and disoriented, because they can neither form themselves into coherent, dignified entities nor lose themselves in wholes greater than themselves.

Ideological societies were based on fanatical imposition of definite answers on individuals miserably worn out by the seemingly unlimited freedom and perpetual questioning of modern life. Individuals today aim at passive serenity by feigning indifference to the answers of fundamental questions. Ideological fanaticism was cruelly, monstrously, and pointlessly destructive of lots of persons. For individuals and individualistic societies, the antidote is relativism. Relativism may be equally opposed to the truth about the question-laden, risk-taking person, but the relativistic alternative has the advantage that nobody gets hurt.

The free individual surrenders the subject's adventure of the uncertain pursuit of the truth and caring harmony with other people. It's not worth the risk; it's more trouble than it's worth. Out of fear of perpetuating useless conflict, he rejects the civilizing inheritance of his culture. His pride is to be so self-sufficient as to have absolutely transcended the need for culture. He retains the right to have any opinion he pleases about his soul, and he accords that right easily to others. Anything anyone knows about the soul, he adds, is both incommunicable and dangerous to communicate. For the contemporary individual, to have rights is to have the freedom to be securely imprisoned in one's own private fantasies. The soul is no longer a subject for human conversation.

Anger at the destruction of particular human beings, Delsol acknowledges, caused by religious and ideological human ideals is legitimate. Destruction ran amok like never before in the twentieth century. Today's defenders of human rights devote themselves to protecting what past idealism destroyed—the bare existence of human beings. We have to stop sacrificing present existence for some imaginary future, degrading this life for illusions about eternity or immortality. We have to stop thinking or doing anything that would cause us to sacrifice the security and enjoyment we can have now. The ontological question of who we are threatens the very fact that each of us *is* right now. We can't and don't have to know *why* each of us is irreplaceable and irreducible to do what we can to continue *to be* as material beings. The question of being, we now know, annihilates being.

So the free individual—allegedly certain of his rights—is supposedly free from cultural prejudices and dangerous conflicts over necessarily elusive meaning. He is perfectly free from the past to define himself for himself, to have his own, unique frame of reference, which he knows he can't impose on or even communicate deeply to others. He certainly doesn't bind himself through shared meaning or caring responsibility for a common world. He works to be connected with others only through voluntary contracts that secure his interests in order that that truth, love, or duty don't cause him to surrender his own judgment. He aims to achieve completeness not by living in harmony with others in the world, but through emotional withdrawal. Because, he claims, judgment is undistorted by social emotions or longings, he thinks clearly about what's best for him as an isolated, material being.

The individual's self-sufficiency means to be free him from all dependency—social, familial, sexual, political, and cultural. Our perception of a need for common worlds comes from our awareness of our finitude; Socrates questioned others because he needed to know the answers to questions we share. The individual aims to experience no such needs. He even refuses to acknowledge his dependence on the institutions of the welfare state for the exercise of his freedom; those institutions exists, he thinks, as a matter of right, and he is free not to think about that to which he is entitled. Thinking of others exclusively in terms of rights spares the individual the tyranny of gratitude.

Delsol shows us in many ways that the individual's judgment that he can do it alone is mistaken. He is certainly wrong to believe that he could maintain even his sanity without a huge number of acts of caregiving from others for which he has not and could not have contracted and which can't be understood according to the logic of consent. He is certainly wrong to believe that he doesn't owe others lots of the same sort of solicitous and generous treatment. He has deluded himself when he believes that human beings have evolved beyond the need—as finite, precarious beings—for collective ventures. The dependencies and duties connected with citizenship and war and churches and families have not really withered away. Political life, for example, is still with us, and it still involves the uncertain clash of different understandings of human meaning and the human good. Our irreducibly political world remains a dangerous place, and that danger is a price we pay for our freedom. It's just not true that we can replace political communities with an abstract or reductionistic humanitarian moralism that will allow each of us to focus on enjoyment or private fantasies in security. That could only happen if death or self-conscious mortality withered away, but then we wouldn't even need to be talking about rights.

Evidence of the individual's greatness is his inability, despite his best efforts, to identify himself and so be satisfied with his merely biological being. He thinks he knows for certain that the death of his body is the end of his being, but he still can't reduce his being to his body. By being discontent with his material being, he shows he is more than a material being. If he were a merely biological being like the other animals, he would be immersed in the social, gregarious life we see among the dolphins and chimps. He wouldn't be repulsed by his contingency and inevitable bodily demise.

The individual's solitary utopianism is, in fact, contrary to nature and potentially a threat to the future of the human species. He can choose to devote himself to losing himself in private fantasies rather than do his social and reproductive duties to his species. Chimps do nothing to try to make themselves eternal or immortal, and contemporary individuals may be the first members of our species to be chimp-like in that sense. In another sense, however, they're less chimp-like than ever: The birth dearth that plagues

Europe is evidence that they're choosing for themselves and against their replacements and so their species, and chimps are incapable of doing that. Contemporary individuals aren't, in fact, free of the human longings that produced eternalizing delusions. The individual, unlike the chimp, has freed himself from such delusions only to fall prey to others.

All the individual really claims to know is that his being (which depends on but is not only his biological being) is the opposite of nonbeing. He thinks he can free himself from every form of dependence but dependence on his body. So he can't help but hate his body and everything that reminds him of the limitations it imposes on him, and he can't see anything good or wonderful in his experiences of limitation. He lacks the resources to give himself any meaning or positive content beyond avoiding personal extinction.

The individual's mirror, as Delsol says, reflects no image. His emptiness is the foundation of the kind of subjection most characteristic of our world. The empty self is really a kind of lobotomized subject who fantastically refuses to be moved by what he really knows. Being lobotomized means being and not being diverted. In one sense, the individual never takes his eyes off the terrible truth he knows about himself. In doing everything he can not to be moved by it, he remains moved by it. The lobotomy never really quite takes.

Recent experience suggests, Delsol observes, that without some conception of eternity or immortality or measureless time human beings can't think of themselves as the irreplaceable and immeasurable wholes they really are. The individual has shown us that as soon as the categories of immortality or eternity disappear human existence becomes fragmented. Individuals abandon the idea of a life-work that is a testimony to their integrity. People used to think that some image of them remained in the mirror, so to speak, even after their bodies disappeared from view. But the individual lacks the resources to generate an image to leave behind. Because he refuses to think of his life as a whole, the individual lives, in a way, through a succession of disconnected deaths. Each of his successive, disconnected projects or "lives" is much more fleeting than the life of a person or subject.

It's the individual's terrified inability to believe in anything beyond himself that's the cause of his increasingly ephemeral existence. He's increasingly defined in some ways by his materialism—by health, safety, comfort, and material productivity, although he finds no enduring satisfaction in material pursuits. He certainly has the right to but lacks what it really takes to engage in independent thought. When all alone with his thoughts, he experiences paralyzing vertigo, and so he's all too ready to work to lose himself in a fashionable crowd. He swings incoherently between his proclaimed relativistic indifference to truth and craven submission to public opinion. His relativism—a reflection of his fragmented inability to find himself or a personal point of view—affords him no protection from either enervating materialism or the reigning moralistic dogmatism. Whether in a relativistic or moralistic mode, he, Delsol observes, suffers from a deteriorated relationship with the truth.

PRODUCTIVITY VS. CAREGIVING

All the individual has to escape dogmatic relativism is the solid ground of measurable productivity as described by economists. Because his self-content is a meaningless private fantasy, the individual can't resist the impersonal and anonymous conclusion that everything real about him can be measured. There's nothing more to him that really deserves to be honored or recognized by others. Our dignity or "public worth," as the individualist Hobbes says, is in our productivity, our ability to be of use to other individuals.[8]

Not so long ago, the activities connected with production were pretty much confined to men, and caregiving was for women and priests. Once medicine, for example, became an intellectual and obviously productive activity—about the real business of saving lots of lives—it became the province of men who got paid for their work. Providing for the basic needs of vigilance, care, friendship and patience—what we all need—seemed to require no official knowledge or special competency. The results of the work were characteristically neither visible nor measurable—or not, strictly speaking, results at all. What caregiving requires and provides can't be captured by the categories of time and profit. Its solicitude and generosity is expressed in an infinite number of simple, personal gestures.

It used to be understood that the seemingly boring and easy work of the caregiver goes unpaid because it's priceless. The sphere of giving and gratitude can't be reduced to the sphere of contractual exchange. It was possible for women and priests (and nuns) to live well enough without wages or even much personal recognition because of the irreducible importance accorded to the activity of caregiving.

Caregiving, finally, is in its way infinitely more important than mere production, because it is more personal. Delsol explains that the seeming banality of the world of caregiving readily connected with the profound wisdom of religious spirituality. The middle-class man achieved his productive accomplishments at the expense of some disconnection from both the mystery of the personal good-ness of ordinary life and the mystery of God. Because there's little mysterious about what works in business and politics, it's easy for those occupied there to forget the mystery of human being.

Surely Delsol's eloquent praise of the personal caregiving of the past must qualify what she generally says about the premodern world. The caregiver didn't regard herself as primarily part of some group or external whole. She was a person who served particular persons. The activity of caregiving is evidence that there's always been personal reality, and spiritual life has always had a personal dimension. That caregiving and spirituality became more personal with the coming of Christianity is surely true, as is the fact that their deterioration is an understandable consequence of modern de-personalization. The unique and irreplaceable activity of the ordinary caregiver must at least qualify the thought that the person or subject must be a dissident. The devoted caregiver is evidence that total immersion in the details of ordinary life might, in fact, be more personal in certain ways that dissident heroism in the face of uncertainty. The ordinary caregiver and the dissident are different manifestations of the complexity of being a person, different ways of caring for the human beings we actually know and love.

Delsol doesn't deny for a moment the advantages of women having the opportunity to enter the productive worlds of business and politics. Excluding them from productive activities was an unjust denial of some their real personal capabilities, but the price of that progress has been the effort to turn caregiving into paid work and redefine human value in terms of measurable results. The new distinction is between being paid and being idle, and there's no dignity in merely being idle. More and more people who aren't productive and can't pay are left out in the cold—delinquent children, the lonely elderly, and all who are poor and vulnerable. The truth is that people—mistakenly thinking of themselves as solitary individuals more and more of the time—are in many way more lonely and so more in need of the solicitude of caregiving than ever. What they most need is held in more contempt than ever.

It makes no sense, of course, to speak of a human right to caregiving. Our undeniable crisis of caregiving is a key piece of evidence of the impossibility of orienting ourselves around human rights with no thought about who we are. The individual mistakenly believes that it's undignified to devote one's life to caring for persons or the institutions on which persons depend. Without that devotion, of course, depersonalization extends even to the raising of children, who go unformed or uncivilized as anything more than productive beings.

DIGNITY AND ORIGINAL SIN

Thinking about the crisis in caregiving—the crisis in confidence that we really are more than productive beings—causes us to wonder to what extent the modern effort to detach the person from any specifically biblical teaching is doomed to failure. Is it possible to become a person without some cultural determination by certainties presented by the Bible? The dignified person, to understand himself, must believe that good and evil are real and personal, and that the dramatic moral adventure of every human life is the inward struggle between good and evil. The Bible recognizes this through the myth of original sin. That sin was the result of the freedom given to each of us, and the possibility of sinning is part of what dignifies each of us. Aristotle also thought, Delsol goes on, that human strife was rooted in human nature, and not caused by the absence of an institutional remedy such as communism. The mystery of freedom for believers was a source of philosophical astonishment for Aristotle. For Aristotle, the enigma of human freedom was the source of the inevitable conflict between partisans, and it was the source of the West's discovery or invention of political life. Political liberty—which is the exception in human history, as despotism or uniform imposition is the rule—has its foundation, for Aristotle, in the natural diversity of opinion and the uncertainty of any solutions. When writing about Aristotle and politics, Delsol makes it clear that the premodern world was not only about the imposition of opinion on people as parts of wholes. A lot—if not everything—about the free and responsible person was discovered with the philosophic articulation of man's political or partisan nature. Aristotelian political life, like the myth of original sin, aims to both protect and display true human diversity and liberty.

Modern thought quickly dismissed the idea of original sin as mere myth and the diversity of political life as a mere social construction. Evil itself was our historical creation and so could have a historical solution. Rousseau, among others, said that our original or pure natures were innocence perfected. So the idea of original sin is a slander against who we really are. We can reasonably work to eliminate evil from this world; the cause of evil can be located and scapegoated. We will be perfect—we will redeem ourselves—through our destruction of the bourgeoisie or the Jews. That Manichean, regressive distinction between historical guilt and perfect innocence is based on denial of the real complexity of every human person. The Rousseauians and the Marxists divided us into angels and demons. That means they reduced everyone to less than he or she is.

The dignity of the personal moral struggle—the fact that it's an irreducible and irreplaceable part of each of our beings—is dissipated by unrealistic historical hopes of bringing it to an end. Under communism, finitude and precariousness will not distort human experience, just as they didn't distort the experience of Rousseau's unconscious or perfectly undignified natural man. Under communism, the life of every human being will be as pointless or weightless as those of the other animals. Actually, human lives will be more meaningless still; they won't even be social beings instinctually doing our duty to the species and serving a natural end.

The genuinely self-aware person/subject thinks that he is the author of what he does. He is capable of being both good and evil, and so he can't reasonably blame society or some collective conception of responsibility for what ails him. Only the facts that we're never entirely innocent nor entirely dependent on forces beyond our control allow us to claim the high status of subject. We're all given the dignified capability to approach personal perfection but we can never actually attain it.

Overcoming Manicheanism, Delsol concludes, requires the recovery of the postulate of an original evil that's part of our dignified condition as free—and so self-consciously finite and precarious—beings. It requires certainty concerning the ubiquity of good and evil. That postulation or certainty, it seems, would require something like Christian belief in the reality of the person—including, of course, personal conscience. Can we say the anti-communist dissidents had at least that much certainty, even without belief in Christian revelation? For them, the myth of original sin was a reflection of who we really are, whether or not the Biblical account of creation is actually true.

PERSONAL VERSUS IMPERSONAL THEOLOGY

Delsol says that persons make a claim for uniqueness because they die as unique beings. But she also doubts that self-conscious mortality is really enough to sustain the person's truthful self-understanding. Delsol claims that the Biblical religion—the religion of personal transcendence—really saved the unique person by extending his unique existence eternally. That belief supported the emergence of the idea of personal conscience, personal responsibility, and the emergence of the modern subject.

The personal religion of the Bible, she explains, was an indispensable contribution to progress toward a true understanding of who each of us is. Personal theology showed us and gave us confidence in the reality of conscious and responsible person as a whole or integrated being. Even Aristotle's God was a principle, not a person. Aristotle's impersonal theological suggestion is that, finally, each of us is an anonymous part of some natural whole. His astonishment at the moral phenomena of good and evil was subordinated to an impersonal idea of eternity that had no place for our moral pretensions.

The Biblical personal relationship between man and God preserves the real integrity of both persons. God and each man know and love each other as persons; neither surrenders his personal identity or judgment to the other. The real question for Delsol is whether our faith in the reality of the human person can survive our skepticism or denial of the reality of the divine person. Can our faith in the human person—and so our confidence in the inalienability of human rights and human dignity—survive without anyone to guarantee what we can't provide for ourselves—continued personal existence after biological death?

Delsol says that the abandonment of personal theology was a key error of the Enlightenment. The human person was left all on his own, without any support from natural or divine reality. With the eighteenth-century advent of Deism, God, once again, became an impersonal principle. The eternal, mechanical laws of nature replaced the providential, personal God. Nature's God, unlike the Biblical God, doesn't care for or even recognize the reality of persons.

We might want to say that the Enlightenment return to Aristotle's impersonal science of nature was on behalf of the truth about the subject as questioner. Certainly any belief in a personal God is, at best, uncertain and faith based, and the modern subject takes no certainty on faith. Delsol herself says in one place that belief in personal eternity devalues the real existence of persons in this world. We should care for persons as we actually know them, and not think of them as more or less than who they really are. We shouldn't sacrifice the precarious beings who live in time to any illusory conception of their immortality or eternity. Thinking of

them as more than who they really are keeps us from caring properly for them as they are, from living as well as we can in the only
world we really know.

So it might be possible to say that the Enlightenment skepticism
concerning the personal God was in the service of real persons. The
premise of the personal, providential God is one way among many
we express the fact that we can't help but find our precariousness
repulsive, that we can't help but long to be more than who we
really are. The person or subject surely aims to overcome that aver-
sion in the name of living in light of the truth. Like Socrates, the
modern subject, it would appear, should affirm the truth that, despite our best efforts, we don't yet know whether or not particular
persons survive biological death. Our view of personal dignity
can't depend on aggressively asserting with certainty what we
don't really know. Surely our unique, irreducible irreplaceability
can't depend on personal immortality. Doesn't it depend, as Delsol
sometimes says, on our knowledge of personal death, which is
actually compromised in those who don't believe that biological
death is real?

Delsol can readily respond that the Enlightenment return to impersonal theology doesn't really serve what we can't help but
know. As a theological view, it is a dogmatic assertion about death
ending the reality of the person and about God and nature being
intransigently indifferent to the person's very existence. The theology of "Nature's God" returns us to the pre-Biblical or Aristotelian
thought that the person is unreal; from the perspective of the truth
about human dignity, it's regression. The (we Americans say)
Lockean individualism of the Enlightenment seems to make the
person or individual responsible for creating himself out of nothing—for literally doing what the Creator allegedly did. Scientific
(for example, Darwinian) doubt about the very reality of the person

came from the complete disconnection between the alleged experience of personal freedom and what we know through science and even theology.

The Enlightenment theology, from this view, seems to be a spin on the Aristotelian observation that particular human beings want to be important or dignified, with an implicit denial that they really are who they want to be. It's no wonder that the Enlightenment so readily morphed into a full-scale rebellion against human finitude. The relentless impersonality of Nature's God is the cause of fanatical historical and technological efforts to defeat death or achieve immortality through our own efforts. And those efforts, of course, are undignified denials of the real foundation of our dignity. Impersonal theology is one cause of the individual's inability to find personal contentment.

The effect of the death of the personal God wasn't to free the human person to be who he is. It turned modernity in the direction of depersonalization. The subject, freed to be wholly on his own, was free for his individualistic dilution and even pantheistic disappearance. The post-Christian modern theology, Delsol explains, is pantheism, the perfectly egalitarian version of impersonal theology. Personal claims for uniqueness or distinctiveness are abolished through dissolving him into a whole that his somehow both homogeneous and divine. We are all indistinguishable parts of the One which is all of being. Pantheism completes the victory of modern equality over modern liberty by revealing that we are nothing more than parts of an undifferentiated whole. Our New Agey, sort of Asian, pantheism is the logical culmination of the victory of modern impersonal science over the pretensions of free persons to be able to sustain themselves all alone in a hostile environment.

The self-effacing oneness of pantheism, of course, is really one display among many of the fearful flight from the truth about the self or the person. Pantheism gives meaning to death as the decisive abolition of the illusions that produced the misery of personal alienation. I am absorbed into the sacralized or divinized whole of which, in truth, I was always nothing more than a part. Pantheism actually claims to abolish the reality of personal death. Because the divine matter of which I am composed can be neither created nor destroyed, what I really am is really immortal. I can become a dolphin or tree as soon as I surrender the illusion that the "I" that I am now will not really be the dolphin or the tree. The only thing that stands in the way of affirming pantheism's truth is the illusion that the self or subject is real, that I am different from and greater than a dolphin or a tree. The emergence of pantheism, deep ecologists say, is a natural antidote to the individual's unsustainable effort to free himself from his natural dependence.

Pantheism, it seems to me, is pretty much a failed lullaby for modern individuals. The individual lacks the resources to be his own whole or have personal integrity. But the individual also can't think of himself as a part of a larger or greater whole. He depends on the dogma that his own death is the extinction of being itself. He can't lose himself in the private fantasy of a pantheistic reverie, even with the help of mood enhancing drugs. He never doesn't know that the tree his matter becomes isn't really him. Modern science and, increasingly, modern theology denies the existence of the individual or person, but they can't eradicate the experience of the individual, which is based on what he knows about his precariousness and his finitude.

The pantheistic or even the Darwinian denial of his alienation from nature can't help but be incredible to him. He may be induced to pray to the One, but he still knows all too well that he himself is, or at least aspires to be, the one. His failed attempts at self-denial are the products of his inability to achieve either successful self-creation or self-destruction. Pantheism reflects both his longing for regression and his longing for immortality, both of which appear to be natural results of what we really know about ourselves. It goes without saying that neither the Deistic God nor the pantheistic One can save anyone in particular. The individual also, of course, does not have the cultural resources to generate the personal self-discipline to experience the complete self-negation that might be the real experience of a true Buddhist.

Because individuals still exist, Delsol says, they still demand human rights, and the real problem with pantheism is that it makes nonsense of such claims. Delsol says that any claim for human rights has to be based on some understanding of the human being that persuasively defends his claim for irreducible uniqueness and irreplaceability. No theology denies that claim more radically than pantheism. Delsol follows Tocqueville in holding that a society full of undifferentiated beings who surrender their liberty—especially their intellectual liberty—to the impersonal, schoolmarmish authority of a meddlesome bureaucracy and/or the anonymous authorities of either public opinion or popularized science would be well served by pantheism.[9] So pantheism would appear to the theology of the abstract universalism of the "humanitarian" or apolitical version of human rights. But if our goal is a society animated by free and self-confident persons or subjects, "the more appropriate partner would be a monotheism that preaches personal eternity, one in which each irreducible being survives in its irreducibility."[10]

What Delsol seems to mean is that those who want to encourage the emergence of the modern person or subject should choose what is preached about what occurs after death. Persons should be preached a certainty that's not, of course, self-evident. Religious and social/political/cultural choices are characteristically interdependent. Delsol doesn't want to say the religious choice is prior to the social or political or vice versa. She doesn't even want to say that religion should be judged only by its utility in preserving our devotion to inalienable human dignity. Social or cultural arrangements can be a product of human choice, but religion—the truth about God and all that—is surely beyond our determination.

Delsol might say that all cultures have been based on some preaching about man's transcendence of his merely biological or temporal existence. The person/ subject knows that such transcendence is real; he can see that the self-consciously finite and precarious being exhibits a dignity or greatness that can't be reduced to the impersonal laws of science. Impersonal science can't account for the mystery of the reality of the human person. Whenever we deny the real existence of that person, we always speak unempirically or abstractly. Those who have said that human beings are merely one part of nature among many or merely part of some social or political whole have always been wrong, although the full understanding of that truth was only made possible by the coming of the personal God of Biblical religion.

The literal belief in personal survival of death is uncertain; anything we say about what happens after death is, for the Socratic questioner, speculative. But that belief reflects what each person in a genuinely personal or dignified culture should think, with plenty of evidence in this world, about his or her unique and immeasurable irreplaceability. Our own experience suggests in many ways that it's more credible than the impersonal theology of "Nature's God." Some persons will always live a somewhat dissident distance from any cultural certainty, but they can still affirm it as a more adequate representation of who we are than the theological alternatives. It's inhuman and undignified to feign indifference to the answers to the theological questions we can't help but raise.

The ontological issue, it turns out, that would have to be resolved for human rights to be rooted securely in a truthful account of human dignity is whether there's a foundation for the human person in the structure of being itself. The contradiction between personal experience and impersonal theology or science may be the deepest source of modern instability, of why the person—or a culture devoted to personal flourishing—has not yet been born. Maybe both the dissidents and the most thoughtful of the Christians[11] have shown us that the experience of personal dignity, thought through, makes personal theology the most credible of the uncertain possibilities.

NOTES

1. These books were published by ISI (Wilmington, DE) in 2008, 2006, and 2003, respectively.

2. Delsol doesn't actually use the phrase "negative Platonism," although it's central to Patocka's thought. See Johann P. Arnason, "The Idea of 'Negative Platonism' in Jan Patocka's Critique and Recovery of Metaphysics," *Thesis Eleven* 90 (2007): 6–26.

3. Alexis de Tocqueville, *Democracy in America*, trans. H. Mansfield and D. Winthrop (Chicago: University of Chicago Press, 2000), 407–410.

4. See Thomas L. Pangle, *Leo Strauss: An Introduction to His Thought and Intellectual Legacy* (Baltimore: Johns Hopkins University Press, 2006).

5. See Vaclav Havel, *Open Letters* (New York: Knopf, 1994) and Aleksandr Solzhenitsyn, *The Solzhenitsyn Reader*, ed. E. Ericson and D. Mahoney (Wilmington, DE: ISI Books, 2006).

6. Walker Percy, *Lost in the Cosmos: The Self-Help Book* (New York: Farrar, Straus and Giroux, 1983) and my *Aliens in America: The Strange Truth about Our Souls* (Wilmington, DE, 2002), 51–74, 251–272.

7. See especially Solzhenitsyn, 561–575, and my "Tocqueville on Magnanimity and Justice," *Magnanimity Ancient and Modern*, ed. C. Holloway (Lanham, MD: Lexington Books, 2008).

8. Thomas Hobbes, *Leviathan*, ed. C. B. Macpherson (New York: Penguin Classics, 1982), chap. 10.

9. See Tocqueville, 407–410, 425–426, 66–73.

10. Delsol, *Unlearned Lessons*, 195.

11. See my "American Nominalism and the Need for a Science of Theology," *Gained Horizons*, ed. B. Cowan (South Bend, IN: St. Augustine's Press, forthcoming).

Chapter Five

The Charms of Indeterminateness

Chantal Delsol on a Democratic and "Late Modern"
Propensity

Carl Eric Scott

In her trilogy on "late modernity," consisting of *Icarus Fallen, The Unlearned Lessons of the Twentieth Century*, and now completed with *Unjust Justice*,[1] Chantal Delsol has given us a work that deserves to attain classic status. The debates certain of her more controversial arguments are bound to provoke, particularly those on international law, may delude some into thinking they can neatly characterize her thought. However, those who attentively read this work will quickly realize, as was once said of Alexis de Tocqueville's *Democracy in America*, that "it contains chapters that are entire books."[2] Indeed, while the differences between her more philosophic mode of sociological analysis and his more directly political mode are significant, a strong case can be made that Delsol is the Tocqueville for our time, the thinker who most deftly illuminates the contemporary situation and what it portends.

This essay focuses on just one of the many ideas Delsol explores, that of *indeterminateness*. Despite the abstraction implied by the term, it refers to a cultural value and pattern we have all become quite familiar with. She says that our era is characterized by a personality who

> prefers liberty to determinateness, which inevitably closes doors. I can become anything if I say that I am nothing definite. . . . Indeterminateness consists in the desire to explore, to refrain from making choices, or rather to choose the possible over the real, the likely over the true, well-being over the good, the moment over time. . . . [It] provides a great euphoria, an illusion of plurality and perfection. (*Unlearned Lessons*, 65)

I am drawn to this particular theme of Delsol's because my own scholarly work has explored, through a comparative study of Tocqueville and Plato, the possibility that there exists a uniquely democratic character shared by the peoples of every democratic polity across the ages, and that its defining feature is *inconstancy*.[3] What I mean by inconstancy is best illustrated by the following passage from book 8 of Plato's *Republic*, in which the "democratic man," due to being ruled by his desires,

> lives along day by day, gratifying the desire that occurs to him, at one time drinking and listening to the flute, at another downing water and reducing; now practicing gymnastic, and again idling and neglecting everything; and sometimes spending his time as though he were occupied with philosophy. Often he engages in politics and, jumping up, says and does whatever chances to come to him; and if he ever admires any soldiers, he turns in that direction; and if it's money-makers, in that one. And there is neither order nor necessity in his life, but calling this life sweet, free, and blessed, he follows it throughout. (561d)

Clearly, this is a lot like indeterminateness. Before returning to Delsol's concept, it will be worthwhile to consider the implications and the contemporary resonance of this passage.

Book 8 is the part of the *Republic* that suggests that there are basically five political regimes and five corresponding ways of private life. In descending order, the ways of life are those of the philosopher, the warrior, the money-maker, the democratic man, and the tyrannical man. Part of what this passage shows us is that the democratic man seeks to be, in turn, each of the other types of men, with the exception of the tyrannical man. His reason for doing so is bound up in his attitude toward the various sorts of pleasure, which he regards as "all alike." He "shakes his head" at those who say "there are some pleasures belonging to fine and good desires and some belonging to bad desires," holding instead that they all "must be honored on an equal basis" (561c). By describing this man, and his eventual enslavement to the desires he unleashes, Plato obviously means to impart a psychological truth about the nature of human desires and why a habituating management of them is necessary. But he also means for us to notice the *ideology* the acceptance of this truth is up against. This ideology holds that every sort of pleasure is equally worthy of pursuit, as is every way of life, albeit with two caveats. First, any pleasure or way of life that harms others is forbidden. Second, a way of life that manages to encompass all the others is actually better than any one of them. Such a life is the most democracy-friendly one, because any man who pursues a way of life that consistently cultivates one sort of excellence likely does so because he thinks it is the supreme one, and it follows that he is liable to think that the best regime is the one ruled by those who exemplify that sort of excellence. This is the logic of every form of aristocracy. Thus, to truly support democracy, says Plato's democratic man, one must live the only life that escapes that logic, the variety-packed one that purports to honor all ways of life.[4]

Despite my speaking of democratic inconstancy, and Delsol of indeterminateness, contemporary debates about this phenomenon have usually been conducted within the parameters suggested by the term *relativism*. The popular adoption of this term has been in many ways useful, but the term itself has limitations, not the least of which is that almost no-one ever owns up to it. Its basic limitation is that it too readily suggests that we should turn to debates within philosophy to settle the issue. But that which is a socio-ideological tendency as much as it is a philosophy can be refuted a thousand times but still become the dominant fact of an era (as Delsol shows with the example of Marxism's career). As we generally encounter relativism it is not an actual epistemology; rather, if Plato is right, it is the intuitive application of the *democratic idea itself*, in its crudest and most radical form, to the living of one's own life and to the ethical claims of others. Plato saw this tendency at work in ancient democracy, retrograde as it was in many ways compared to ours. Tocqueville also saw it beginning to unfold in American democracy and French republicanism, despite other cultural features that in his day restrained its influence.

Delsol agrees with the basic point here. She uses *procedural tolerance* as an equivalent term to relativism, reminding us that contemporary liberal thought has often been criticized as reducing liberal democracy to nothing but a set of procedures whereby the maximum amount of equal autonomy for individuals can be obtained (*Icarus Fallen*, 125).[5] For her, this further indicates that "in reality, contemporary democratic thinking does not manifest relativism, for it rests on a profound conviction of its own truth" (*Icarus Fallen*, 99).

However, we must notice that Delsol talks of "contemporary" or "late modern" character more often than she does of *democratic* character. In *Icarus Fallen*, for example, she dedicates an entire chapter to the "morality of complacency," which she characterizes as one of the two basic features of "the morality of our time" (65).

Even though we easily recognize the echo of Plato's democratic man in the "complacent man" being predisposed "to seek pleasure" (65) and becoming "a slave to what pleases him" (66), as well as in this "ethics of complacency" being "an openness to all that is possible" that decides "in advance that nothing can be called deviant or unnatural" (67), Delsol does not make the connection to Plato, nor, more importantly, does she apply the word *democratic*. Rather, she presents the morality of complacency as being adopted by "contemporary man," the "contemporary individual," or "our contemporary," and suggests that its promotion of a seeming "open-mindedness" reflects a "modern model" that is "historically unique" (67). Perhaps to understand her thought we need to attend to complacency itself and its relation to contemporary modernity more than we need to consider its relation to the democratic. And yet, in the book's later discussions of contemporary democracy, its tendency to reject "reflection about the foundations of the democratic 'good'" in favor of the "self-evidence" of its production of happiness shows that "it is a politics of complacency, which mirrors the ethics of complacency" (99–100). Both the politics and the ethics justify themselves not by reason but by a feeling of well-being and pleasure, even if it is not clear whether the politics causes the ethics, or vice versa. The *connection* between the democratic and the indeterminate remains, but the shaping of the indeterminate mainly by the democratic, which is plainly asserted by Plato's account, is only indirectly suggested by Delsol's.

This is why a careful examination of Delsol's thought on this whole subject promises a richer understanding of it in general. Thus far, we can see that to grasp the phenomenon of contemporary inconstancy or indeterminateness we must connect it to the democratic idea, which shifts the analysis from *relativism* to the broader topic of *democratic character*. Admittedly, this emphasis on the democratic dimension of the topic poses problems of its own.

First, this emphasis increases the possibility of divisive mis-understanding. Unless "democratic" is understood in Plato's radical manner, there is a danger that those who agree with his critique will too freely apply it to modern liberal democracy; this can lead others to suspect that acceptance of the critique necessarily suggests a desire to replace or undermine our democracy. (Similar problems arise with Tocqueville's complex use of "democratic," despite his open declaration of "critical friendship" toward democracy.) Second, my sense is that what Plato had his finger on in his presentation of the change-embodying democratic character is a perennial temptation of the human condition, that to some degree can operate apart from the political fortunes of the democratic idea. For example, it is from Blaise Pascal's quite apolitical and history-indifferent *Pensées* that I take the term "inconstancy." In doing so I follow Tocqueville's example, as *Democracy in America's* Pascal-influenced discussion of "restlessness" briefly utilizes the term "inconstancy." That discussion shows us that modern democratic conditions unleash the inconstancy the human psyche has always been inherently inclined to—that described by Pascal—by removing the aristocratic conditions and custom-bound horizons that once kept this endemic disease partly in check.[6] That is, Tocqueville gets us to consider the operation of a timeless human trait, inconstancy, within an unfolding human story that by his account has become an ever-more democratic one. He would thus agree with Delsol that "man, even if he does always retain certain characteristics, is a metamorphic rather than a static species" (*Icarus Fallen*, 133).

This begins to show why I am arguing that Delsol's account of indeterminateness, which seems both linked to *the democratic* and potentially independent of it, and likewise both linked to *our contemporary situation* and potentially independent of it, provides us with a fresh and multidimensional view of this subject. Relativism and the democratic encouragement of inconstancy are topics that remain on the table, but let us see if we can approach them in a different manner.

The concept that organizes Delsol's trilogy is *late modernity*. This term describes both our overall culture and our way of thinking about mankind's place in the world. (This culture and thinking are generally Western, especially Western European, and have been adopted to various degrees by the more modernized populations around the world.) Alongside the great philosophic questions— What are we? What is virtue? What can we know?—necessarily comes the question: *Where* are we? That is, where do we stand with respect to the long human effort to understand ourselves and our world? Delsol begins with the following recognition: We are the humans who know that the ideocratic politics enacted in the last century (of which communism was the model, even for many features of National Socialism)[7] did not work and that they worked only horror upon humanity. Further, most of us see that the weaker reflections of the ideocratic dreams in the progressive visions of welfare-state socialism, and later on in various New Left awakenings of cultural revolution, have not really solved the problems they promised to, or have simply brought about newer ones. Delsol likens our situation to that of a man who, like Icarus, thought he could fly up to the sun but now finds himself fallen back upon the earth. Unlike Icarus, this man must continue on with life. This means he must fundamentally reassess his capabilities, even though the lingering hold of his old aspiration makes this a very painful task. The most fundamental conclusion of the needed reassessment is as follows: Although the utopian visions of the twentieth century assumed that man is inherently malleable, the attempt to implement those visions revealed that he is not. We thus can know, upon anthropological reflection informed by this history, that there are

limits to what can be attempted in the reformation of human society, and that these proceed from a set of features that constitute
human nature itself.

Delsol does not think, as we have already glimpsed, that human
nature may be grasped once and for all and then expounded in an
authoritative body of natural laws or natural rights. Rather, it can
only be dimly understood, and only through the distorting lenses of
clashing customs and politicized human events. Her model is Montesquieu. He represents an openness to and a respect for the different approaches to the key human questions embodied by different
communities; significantly, she insists his sort of respect and openness is *not* relativistic. He represents the spirit of cautious and
skeptical *early modernity*, which preceded the spirit of *ideological
modernity* that took flight leading up to and following the French
Revolution. He represents, in other words, modern political pru-
dence. In *Unjust Justice*, she poses his example explicitly against
today's trans-nationalist champions of international justice and human rights, but I think also implicitly against those conservatives
who would seek to force a choice between relativism and natural
law narrowly understood.

We late-moderns are thus the humans who must return to the
early modern spirit, who must rehabituate ourselves to thinking
about human (and cultural) limits, and to resituating our quests for
improvement within those limits. This will involve a continuous
struggle; and, it will require us to resist the universalist and fundamentalist temptations of what she calls a "return to essentialism"
(*Icarus Fallen*, chap. 4). But our more frontal struggle will be
against our ingrained utopian habits. The spiritual energies imparted to us by the now-discredited ideocratic dreams continue to
churn, and to the extent we fail to re-channel them, several possibilities exist. We might (1) simply refuse to learn the lessons taught
by the twentieth century, (2) draw incorrect lessons, (3) come to
only bitter half-acceptance of the new situation, or (4) even to seek

to deny it. Providing a taxonomy of these four possibilities sketched by Delsol will bring us to a place where we can grasp why she holds that we contemporary humans are the ones particularly drawn to indeterminateness.

First, quite a few of us still hold a half-articulated faith in the indefinite progress of mankind; if forced to say something about communism and Nazism, we treat them as authoritarian distortions of this faith or as totally unrelated to it. Among the various things that the enthusiasm for Barack Obama signified, one surely is the existence of a widespread longing to return to the days of boldly progressive visions. His invocation of Change and Audacious Hope illustrated his intuitive detection and expression of this longing.

Second, many add to this basic progressive faith the somber note that what was most fundamental about communism and Nazism was not their banking on the malleability of man, but rather their acceptance of an authoritative answer. As Delsol explains,

> The Inquisition is taken to be the ancestor of all modern totali-
> tarianisms, which have always involved sacrificing men to a
> dogma, or to a triumphant truth. And if we must find a common
> denominator shared by forms of totalitarianism, it must be certi-
> tude itself: this is what we believe we have learned. Certitude
> kills, irrespective of whether it is truth or error that nourishes
> it. . . . Truth, or rather the belief that one possesses the truth, is
> inherently dangerous. (*Icarus Fallen*, 47)

Again and again, Delsol stresses the way in which this *false lesson* of the twentieth century pervades late modernity. It involves a "re-fusal to even go looking for foundations, for fear of actually discovering them" (*Icarus Fallen*, 58). Thus, even many who understand that relativism is self-contradictory and that post-twentieth-century faith in open-ended progress really is naive become willing to promote widespread acceptance of both, as lesser evils that prevent the far worse one of certitude about human nature.

A Plato-informed critique of Delsol at this point might say that this *false lesson*, supposedly best characterized as late modern, actually reveals itself to be inherently democratic. That is, genuine horror at the Holocaust and the Gulag were utilized by the democratic instincts of the contemporary West, so that all too predictably, the lesson taken from Auschwitz and Solvetsky was: *be like the democratic man*. While this critique is true to an extent, I think Delsol would say it is too focused upon classical regime analysis. She stresses, by contrast, the way in which the people of our day are deeply shaped by the human *story* that they believe has been unfolding in a hopeful direction since the Enlightenment. That direction is not simply toward greater political freedom, but toward greater science, greater civilization, greater well-being, greater horizons of opportunity for all, and finally, greater rejection of what Thomas Jefferson called "monkish ignorance." Faith in this unfolding story replaces, or at least overshadows, the older (but *not* classical) faith in the Christian story. Thus, contrary to what classical regime analysis would suggest, contemporary democratic man is less affected by an idolized good of freedom and its embodiment in an ideal democratic life, and more by the ongoing story of progress. For him, it is not too much to say that in this story are met *the hopes and fears of all the years*. And Delsol's argument indicates that we should especially say something about the fears. If the non-naive partisan of progressivism recognizes that the hope for a progressivist "heaven" has been dashed, or at least has become extended so far into the future as to be only personally worked for by a painfully slow and compromise-ridden gradualism, he is absolutely certain that the progressivist vision of "hell" remains grimly relevant. That hell would be the return, likely by populist means, of an essentialist and probably Christianized certitude. Perhaps even worse than the oppression and superstition he is certain such certitude would promote, would be its portrayal of mankind as fated to remain within a truncated horizon of political possibility. He thus urges the denigration of all aspirations to holistic truth, whatever the price to sound philosophy or meaningful liberal education.

According to Delsol, the real outcome of such denigration is the contemporary situation in which the "morality of complacency" triumphs, a situation quite similar to Plato's democratic one. Late modernity's dutiful antagonism toward certitude thus seems to bring us to a place where Plato's account of the democratic soul fully applies to the dominant character type of our day. This suggests, as we shall see, that faith in the *story* of Progress might in our day become replaced by devotion to the *archetype* of the individual's indeterminate Freedom.

The third possibility for us late moderns, which may surely work with the others, is that in revulsion at the limitations revealed by our post-twentieth-century situation, we become embittered, and choose to distance ourselves from all hopes by means of *derision*. An aggressive sort of ridicule, which was once purposefully employed by the ideocratic movements against the cultural habits they intended to advance beyond, comes to serve a psychological need. On this topic, it is best to quote Delsol at length:

> Modern man thought he saw . . . the perfect beauty of the Good, glimpsed in a rare moment, then instantly gone. The loss seems unbearable. The lover takes to wandering in a world where nothing pleases him anymore. This is how so many former disciples of communism look, marked as they are by what Central and Eastern Europeans call the "Hegelian bite." . . . He begins to hate this world, which has revealed itself to be incapable of achieving the Good. He blocks it out, preferring not to see its mediocrity. Thus can we explain the bitterness, resentment, and rancor harbored by the present era. (*Unlearned Lessons*, 35–36)

All wind up on the receiving end of this bitterness, but some targets particularly attract its scorn:

It is like the passionate participant in the events of May 1968 who advocated an upbringing and schooling in which nothing is forbidden—one aspect of the utopia of progress—and then later suddenly realizes that his children obey no creed or law. When his error finally dawns on him, he realizes that it is much too late to change anything: he prefers then to discredit what he does not have rather than to recognize the harmful consequences of his theories. He methodically ridicules any form of education other than his own, pointing out flaws that predictably manifest themselves everywhere. . . . The widespread ridiculing of traditional rearing and education practices often stems from this kind of unspoken unhappiness. (*Unlearned Lessons,* 36–37)

With this man, retreats from earlier errors are never acknowledged as such, and he thus leads a life that contradicts the constant theme of his tongue:

He leads an upper-middle-class life, but relentlessly disparages the middle-class; he runs things as though he were a free-market advocate, but jeers at free-market ideas. . . . [H]e continues to propagate the utopia he no longer lives by, and attacks the moralism of those who simply put into words what he himself is doing. (*Unlearned Lessons,* 37)

It is a most unattractive picture, and all the more so because it is apparent that this type of person has been setting much of the tone of our politics and culture for some time. The way this works in America differs from the way it does in Western or Eastern Europe, but the basic applicability is clear enough. It does much, in my opinion, to explain the otherwise peculiarly histrionic and vicious season of political speech provoked by the electoral victories of George W. Bush, as well as the lamentably more intransigent fact that since sometime in the 1990s many of us have taken to talking as if we were trapped on the set of *Saturday Night Live,* forever ridiculing, ironic, and filth-insinuating. Generations who never held the utopian faiths that first inculcated the habit of derision have picked it up, so that it has become second nature for many late modern persons.

The fourth possibility is that hatred of the post-twentieth-century situation is taken to the level of outright denial and escapism. Indeterminateness is the ultimate form of this, but there are many others. Delsol mentions drug-centered alternate-reality creation as a particularly attractive form, and she dwells upon a contemporary sort of stoicism designed to trim all hopes down to the minimum. She connects both of these to the general growth of bond-avoiding individualism:

> And in many cases, we prefer to avoid a feeling, or reject an institution, rather than to live in the mediocrity that they reflect. Turn-of-the-century individualism feeds on a weariness with the kind of interpersonal relationships that give rise to dependence and quarreling, carry the risk of disappointment, and demand concession and patience. If to bond with another person turns out to be so complex . . . then it is better to be alone, free, and without any expectations at all. (*Unlearned Lessons*, 42)

But this is not the end of the story. One may turn to indeterminateness, which seems to be an individualistic way to reclaim modern idealism. Delsol speaks of a "contemporary freedom" that legitimates "experimentation upon oneself, on the condition that it is voluntary" (*Unlearned Lessons,* 40). Moreover,

> The contemporary individual believes he is capable of inventing whatever it is he wants to be . . . in this sense he has inherited that ideology which thought it could reinvent humanity. . . . Contemporary individualism represents the continuation, in solitary form, of the utopian dream. (*Unlearned Lessons*, 60)

However, whereas the twentieth-century utopians advocated experimentation with man and his social organization in order to scientifically arrive at an undeniably better society, the devotee of indeterminateness is a dedicated individualist, and what is more, one who does not mean to arrive anywhere. There is no expectation that the next self-experiment will bring one to something undeniably better or closer to an ultimate goal. There is no better or worse state of life, only more or less variability embraced by one's life. Of course, since there are only so many human possibilities, then like Plato's democratic man the self-experimenter eventually finds himself in a broadly cyclical pattern. There is a person who regards this Whitman-esque encompassment of plurality as the best life; he is the one captivated by the "illusion" of "plurality and perfection" of which Delsol speaks. But there is another contemporary sort who poignantly asks, in the words of a recent rock song, *how come I wind up where I started?*

The question is poignant because it shows that indeterminateness is actually a confinement of idealism. One is totally freed, but only to arrive at total freedom. One may become "interested in" any particular culture or way of life whatsoever, but one must not make the mistake of thinking that any one of them provides a genuine guide to life. We travel. We party. We work out. We make money. We spend money. Made indignant at some patent abuse viewed on television, or alarmed by some movement making pretensions to know the "truth," we "become involved" with our tongues afire. When too frustrated, we "drop out." We rebel. We rebel against our last rebellion. We take a tour through "the world of ideas," and then perhaps through that of "spirituality." We celebrate the *strange ch-ch-changes* of our lives. With each of us thus encased in our own ever-turning kaleidoscopic sphere, our denial of the collapse of the progressive dream can become complete.

Such willful blindness to human needs for restraints, and for sustained passions as well, obviously results in poorly lived lives. But perhaps the more effective objection is that indeterminateness actually kills the progressive vision it seeks to vindicate. While it loudly touts Change and insists upon the malleability of the human, it discards all theism-like emphasis upon the hopeful story, and replaces it with a pantheism-like vision of the individual democratically representing, and thus containing, the All. It does so to exhibit the individual's freedom, and yet it has nothing to say against the insistence, which consistent pantheist logic joins with consistent materialist logic in making, that freewill is illusory, as is the individual's genuine distinction from the All. Thus, in the rare instances when it is thought through, the embrace of indeterminateness cannot be a conviction of hope. It must rather be a resigned acceptance of the conclusion that only the *illusions* of selfhood and freedom allow "oneself" to avoid the experience of profound unhappiness, and only when they are used to equally accept all cosmic possibilities and to equally emulate all human ones.

This strategy of illusion-acceptance-and-management has the added benefit of protecting human society from a return to fundamentalist certitude, the mere prospect of which deeply disturbs contemporary man, although it is not clear why it should since by his usual lights whatever happens will be determined by the interactions of genes and memes anyhow. Why get upset about the prospect that one illusion system will triumph over another? That is, why care that a fundamentalist system would be less able (according to this reasoning) to divert humans from their sad lot? Could it be that for the maximum level of happiness humans also need another sort of illusion, that of an *enemy*? So that contrary to what we might expect, non-fundamentalist humans need this as much as any others do? So that they would need not only indeterminate freedom, but also the *cause* of anti-fundamentalism? Perhaps, then, we can understand why even indeterminateness, so given to complacency, is also given to seasons of political outrage. Throughout her trilogy Delsol shows us the various ways in which this oscillation between a relaxed relativism, on the one hand, and a passionate political Manichaeism, on the other hand, has become a regular feature of our late-modern situation.

Chinua Achebe has a character of his say, "Writers don't give prescriptions; they give headaches!" Chantal Delsol is not one of those writers. She offers an alternative to the late-modern approach to life, but one that is not an attempt to return to pre-modernity nor an acceptance of essentialist fundamentalism. It is founded on her development of a philosophic anthropology—to learn about that, one must turn to the trilogy itself, but here we can take a glimpse at the alternative way of life Delsol poses against the indeterminate one. She calls it the "authentic subject," and models it on the stubborn bravery of East-European dissidents. Such a subject

> brings his weight to bear on the world in order to change it, risks his being in moral decision-making. . . . [He] puts himself on the line so that he can demonstrate that he really is what he is not yet known to be. . . . [He] accepts the discomfort of his paradoxes. He knows himself to be structured because his being is incomplete. . . . [I]n contrast to the contemporary individual, the authentic subject knows himself to be not self-founded, but founded on a debt: the culture that has preceded him promises and permits him the status of subject. (*Unlearned Lessons,* 116, 120)

He does not see himself as determined, as in pantheism and scientism; as importantly, he does not "regard himself as solely the work of the self . . . as in contemporary existentialism" (*Unlearned Lessons,* 121). Unlike the "self-founded subject" who "believes he already possesses everything," the authentic subject regards himself as "a gift that he himself must complete" (*Unlearned Lessons,* 120–21). Ultimately, Delsol suggests that man cannot believe this unless he is open to the possibility of a Giver above and beyond every culture.

While a full treatment of Delsol's thought thus requires investigation of her use of the concept of "subject" that comes out of particular currents in modern philosophy, and of her thought's relation to Christian theism, the overall shape of her account of indeterminateness should by now be fairly clear. We have seen that her approach both sheds new light on current debates about relativism and its causes, and contains echoes of Plato, Tocqueville, and Pascal. Those echoes indicate, in my judgment, that the human attraction to indeterminateness is a perennial trait, even if it is one which has become particularly strong in our extra-democratic and late-modern era. That is, I hold that indeterminateness must be explained by all three of the following factors: (1) democracy, (2) modernity (whether early, ideological, or late),[8] and (3) perennial human discontents and aspirations. Insofar as Delsol's discussion holds that modernity is the real key, it is in that sense limited. But as some of the quotations presented above suggest, she seems quite aware of the other two influences. In any case, hers is the work that most vividly conveys how the ideal of indeterminateness is increasingly becoming a basic characteristic of and ruling standard for contemporary society, and thus, why greater understanding of its charms is urgently needed.

NOTES

1. Chantal Delsol, *Icarus Fallen: The Search for Meaning in an Uncertain World* (Wilmington, DE: ISI Books, 2003); *The Unlearned Lessons of the Twentieth Century: An Essay on Late Modernity* (Wilmington, DE: ISI Books, 2006); *Unjust Justice: Against the Tyranny of International Law* (Wilmington, DE: ISI Books, 2008).

2. Hugh Brogan, *Alexis de Tocqueville: A Life* (New Haven, CT: Yale University Press, 2006) 293, quoting Narcisse-A. Salvandy's 1835 review of *Democracy in America*.

3. See Carl Eric Scott, "The Inconstant Democratic Character: A Comparison of Plato's *Republic* and Tocqueville's *Democracy in America*" (PhD dissertation, Fordham University, 2008) esp. chaps. 1 and 3.

4. In holding this view, Plato's democratic man has plenty of modern democratic company. John Dewey holds that "a notion that inherently some realities are superior to others, are better than others . . . inevitably works on behalf of a regime of authority." Dewey, *The Political Writings of John Dewey*, ed. Debra Morris and Ian Shapiro (Indianapolis, IN: Hackett, 1993), 45. Or consider this exposition of Walt Whitman's thought by contemporary democratic theorist

Morton Schoolman: "Democracy is 'adjusted to time and space' by way of an aesthetic receptivity to the world that, inclusive of universality's diversity of differences, includes *at any one time* all the time and space belonging to universality's diverse forms of life." That is, the good democrat will imitate Whitman's "receptivity," his deliberate effort in his poetry and life to "contain multitudes." Schoolman, *Reason and Horror: Critical Theory, Democracy, and Aesthetic Individuality* (New York: Routledge, 2001), 245 and 240, respectively.

Whitman and Dewey are patron saints for those like Richard Rorty who seek to articulate a *leftist* stance in a broadly post-Marxist manner, although many thinkers who identify themselves as *liberal* speak similarly. Consider the following critical characterization offered by theorist (and self-identified liberal) William Galston: "Contemporary liberal thinkers . . . such as John Rawls, Ronald Dworkin, Bruce Ackerman, and Charles Lamore insist that the state must be 'neutral,' not simply toward religious professions but toward all individual conceptions of the good life. Indeed, they regard this neutrality as the defining characteristic of liberal orders" (Galston, *Liberal Purposes: Goods, Virtues, and Diversity in the Liberal State* [New York: Cambridge University Press, 1991], 7.) Unlike Schoolman, these thinkers do not necessarily claim that the diversity-and-change-embodying life is the best one, but their version of liberalism would have to regard those who sought out such a life as the safest citizens a liberal state could ask for. That is, if these liberal intellectuals are too cautious to be *for* the inconstant democratic man, then they do earn the dubious honor of being the ones *least opposed to* him.

5. See also Michael Sandel, *Democracy's Discontent: America in Search of a Public Philosophy* (New York: Basic Books, 1996); and Philippe Bénéton, *Equality by Default: An Essay on Modernity as Confinement,* (Wilmington, DE: ISI Books, 2004).

6. See Scott, chap. 5 in this volume, and Peter Lawler, *The Restless Mind: Alexis de Tocqueville on the Origin and Perpetuation of Human Liberty* (Lanham, MD: Rowman & Littlefield, 1993).

7. For a good discussion of the evidence for and the limits of this claim, see Pierre Manent's chapter on Nazism in his *A World beyond Politics? A Defense of the Nation-State* (Princeton, NJ: Princeton University Press, 2006). See also Alain Besançon, *A Century of Horrors: Communism, Nazism, and the Uniqueness of the Shoah* (Wilmington, DE: ISI Books, 2007). On "ideology" and "ideocracy," see Daniel Mahoney, *Aleksandr Solzhenitsyn: The Ascent from Ideology* (Lanham, MD: Rowman & Littlefield, 2001).

8. These are Delsol's stages of modernity; they do not necessarily parallel other well-known divisions of modernity, such as Leo Strauss's "three waves of modernity."

Chapter Six

Roles, Functions, and Subsidiarity

Delsol and the Politics of the Contemporary Family

Lauren K. Hall

The family has been the proverbial thorn in the side of political thinkers from Plato to Marx. Philosophers seem not to know what to do with this collection of people brought together by chance, held together by affection and necessity, who create a bond separate and distinct from loyalty to the state. The family stymies rationalistic approaches to the world since it falls into a nether region between choice and coercion, the passions and reason, and most importantly between the individual and the community. In part due to its intermediate position between the individual and the community, the family is one of the foundations for political moderation, forcing upon us the limitations on values like equality and freedom inherent in human life. The family creates individuals and cares for its own, which makes it the crucible of inequality. The family alienates itself from the other side of the political spectrum by binding us, without our consent, to an intergenerational compact, and forcing upon us laws, norms, and conventions to which we do not and realistically cannot consent.

Early liberals like Locke and Hobbes tend to ignore the family and focus on the individual, while communitarian theorists like Marx emphasize the eradication of the family to achieve the equality of the final state. It is not surprising then that the family is most appreciated by those moderate political thinkers who have tried to balance the varied and stringent values of human life.

It is on the edges of classical liberalism that we find the family appreciated for the foundational role it plays in the political order. Ancient thinkers like Aristotle lead the way for more modern political theorists like Burke, Montesquieu, and Tocqueville who all appreciate the importance of the binding character of family life. Each of these thinkers in turn has influenced contemporary thinkers like Chantal Delsol, who uses more ancient teachings to react to the peculiar circumstances of the twentieth century. This chapter deals with Delsol's understanding of political moderation and uses her work as a spring board for a more explicit defense of the family as the grounding for political moderation.

Delsol does not treat the family at length in her translated works, but her defense of particularity forms the basis for a valuable lesson in the importance of family life for political life. Moreover, the extension of her thought supports the belief that where the family fails, the state must and will step into the breach. The replacement of political for familial leads to centralization of power, isolation of individuals, and the replacement of what Delsol calls human "roles" with simple functions or tasks to be carried out by indiscriminant persons. This movement is in line with the modern project of technocracy Delsol criticizes, and leads, if left long enough, to a society composed of last men, creatures whose comfort filled life is devoid of richness or depth of experience. The family may well be the last great barrier to this degraded state.

CRUCIBLE OF INDIVIDUALITY

The family is changing in fundamental ways, and these changes are driven by a combination of social pressure for equality, growth of government power, and economic necessities of a changing techno-logically driven world. Delsol describes this shift: "The common vision of the family based on father- and mother-hood is giving way to a preapproved pattern of tribal relationship, devoid of hier-archy and durable, exclusive bonds."[1] These durable, exclusive bonds that the new family forgoes are the usual foundation for defenses of the family. The family teaches us emotional attach-ment, and in tying us to a family thus ties us to the greater society. The natural bonds that tie family members together are strength-ened by time, necessity, and other external factors, and these most foundational of social ties might even be considered the foundation for human sympathy.[2] Burke perhaps makes the best statement of this principle: "To love the little platoon we belong to in society, is the first principle (the germ as it were) of publick affections."[3]

The family is not only the place where we create enduring bonds and practice social emotions. It is also the place where our individ-uality is allowed to mature. The intense sociality of family life forces a child both inward and outward at the same time. The child who at one moment clings to his mother is at the next moment demanding equal rations with his siblings. The family is our first school for justice, impartiality, reciprocity, and the other moral rules we must learn as individuals. As we quickly learn in family life, affection and attachment are never enough. Despite the pro-found sociality of family life, we are still individuals, and individu-al self-interest and our peculiar talents and desires require that, like in society at large, we create rules of conduct and laws of family life that make the experience of living closely with numerous other individuals possible. Thus family life, while it grooms us in emo-tional attachment and affection, also prepares us for our eventual exit into society; we will have learned the relevant social norms, manners, and customs that prepare us for the conflicts among individuals inherent in human social life. The family successfully mixes the two primary characteristics that make for successful citizenship: emotional attachment to the group and a hearty respect for rule of law, grounded in respect for the individual.

The family also fosters individuality because the family is the only "society" small enough to be able to successfully implement the maxim "to each according to his ability." Children are not expected to be identical, and their differences and talents are taken into account when parents make decisions about how to allocate resources. The small, close-knit family is the only society in which this kind of individual attention to the needs, wants, and talents of individuals can have fair play. Delsol's discussion of roles and functions helps illustrate the way in which the family supports individuality: "A role is conferred in advance, often inscribed in the destiny of the individual, and inalienable. A function is chosen by the individual, is exterior to him, and he appears interchangeable in that function."[4] The family fosters individuality because the family is a society of roles (it may be the only society solely made of roles). Children are not interchangeable, and parents serve different purposes. Our mothers fulfill our needs in a different way than fathers can, providing a different kind of emotional attachment and comfort. The structure of the family is also, ultimately, about roles rather than functions: "A society of roles is hierarchical and differentiated. A society of functions tends towards equality and homogeneity."[5] The family is the crucible of individuality and, therefore, of inequality.

Because family members fill a role and are not interchangeable with each other, members are required to acknowledge their position in the familial hierarchy. They are unequal individuals who, moreover, do not choose their roles in the family and cannot, even through merit, change their roles in that particular family. Even after the death of a parent or having children of one's own, one is still someone else's child. Of course, over the course of generations, one can have numerous roles, which is one element of the rich fabric of human life. One can be a child one moment, and a mother the next, but one can never change one's place in the original family hierarchy. Throughout life one moves through roles, participating in unique relationships with various individuals that are never freely chosen, and which are all fundamentally unequal.

The family limits freedom in a more obvious way; apart from a few situations (adoption and marriage), we are not able to choose our family members. This strikes many as a fundamental injustice, since nice people get saddled with vicious relatives, and vice versa. Pierre Manent refers to this as a final triumph of nature—we have chosen to control if and how many children we have, but we have not (yet) figured out how to choose our children. Even choosing some of the traits of our children does not do away with the fundamental contingency of being powerless over to whom you are born. The uncontrollable linkage that binds us from birth to complete strangers who may or may not be virtuous people is often cited as one of the fundamental injustices in human life.

Modern utopians of all stripes seek to eradicate both the inequality of the family and its determinism. If the community takes the place of the family, we will replace the roles of the family with functions. Mothers and fathers become daycare workers and children become paying customers or wards of the state. Children are treated equally and care workers are paid the same. At the same time, we get to choose the kinds of functions we want (unlike choosing whose daughter to be), and being a daycare worker or a paying customer always assumes a kind of freedom to escape and do something different. Functions provide freedom and equality, while the family provides neither.

THE POLITICAL FAMILY

The family is not simply the place where individuals become differentiated and where inequality and determinism begin. The family plays a more important theoretical role in political life than simply the creation of good citizens or a limiting factor on utopian values. The family is a middle ground between the individual and the community, the particular and the universal. The family exposes the individual to others who are still, in a fundamental way, part of us—it provides us with a solid link between ourselves as individuals and other people. Our parents are not us, but they are not quite completely distinct individuals. This central location between the particular and the universal, between the individual and the social, forces the family into the center of some of the most vicious arguments in the political realm. As the meeting point between community and individual, the family is the logical point of departure for those who value the community or the individual over all other values. Political philosophers like Locke and Hobbes, who want to emphasize the decisions of individual will, downplay the role of the family as the thing that ties individuals inextricably to the political order. The family, in a very real sense, prevents us from giving our consent because it refutes the state of nature that is at the heart of contract theory. There is no state of nature where individuals roam freely. Individuals are chained to the community by familial shackles.

Instead of a state of nature, the family acts as the defining link in an intergenerational compact that ties us to our past and to the future. This compact limits both our individual and societal horizons. Instead of being free to envision and create society out of whole-cloth, we are tied to the imperfect fragments of history that come to us through the history of our nation and our people. The intergenerational compact is most explicitly laid out in Burke, and the importance of the compact is not necessarily its binding character but that it is the way in which we hand down the "particular" to our children. Instead of being simple individuals, ready to soak up whatever comes our way, we are anchored from birth in a particular culture and tradition. The family acts as this anchor, both in historical time and societal space. We are anchored to the history of our nation and people just as we are to our specific society with cultures, traditions, and norms. Anchors serve an important purpose; they prevent ships from being swept away by the waves. They also restrict movement. An anchored ship is not free.

Similarly, political movements that seek to emphasize the importance of the community are struck by the way in which the family creates inequality and, more importantly, a hierarchical ranking of benevolence that some find oppressive. The family creates inequalities in wealth and power which are politically problematic for egalitarians. The family creates inequalities of opportunity and education, which fuels the political problem of unequal power while at the same time appearing to be a serious injustice. The family, perhaps even more importantly, prevents the existence of universal benevolence or love of the community that egalitarians believe is possible. Born into, raised, and nurtured by mothers, fathers, and siblings, the individual treats the family as a sanctuary, next to which political questions and loyalties usually come second. Adam Smith discusses these human propensities for unequal regard as part of our natural sentiments and incapable of being uncoupled from human nature, arguing that family members "are naturally and usually the persons upon whose happiness or misery his [the individual's] conduct must have the greatest influence."[6] Moreover, Smith makes the radically conservative statement that it is not simply the case that we care more for the family than for other people but that this is characteristic of the human condition and is therefore unalterable: "The care of the universal happiness of all rational and sensible beings is the business of God and not of man."[7] Yet utopians often cherish the belief that destruction of the family will result in the group replacing the family as the center around which human emotional life revolves.

Generally, those who value universal values like equality or freedom above all else find the family a stifling reminder of our imperfection. While utopians of all stripes reach out to universals, the family keeps us rooted in the particulars of time and place, preventing radical social progress. The particular encapsulates language, religion, philosophy, politics, law, manners, mores, and general social norms. It also represents archaic traditions, prejudice and discrimination rooted in history, and old ideas and ancient religious beliefs that hold the human mind in place, limiting movement. All political philosophy is characterized by the conflict between the particular and the universal; Delsol's work is instructive because she recognizes the tension between the two but does not feel the need to resolve it.

One of the Delsol's most telling discussions of this tension is her condemnation of international law, which relies heavily on Montesquieu's work on the role of the particular as the foundation for political life. Utopians and international law proponents believe that the more encompassing our benevolence, the better off we are. These idealists believe that there is a kind of absolute truth that is accessible without reference to particular societies and peoples. Delsol uses Montesquieu as a foil to the universalist tendency, arguing that humans are necessarily rooted in the particular. She locates her argument around two major convictions. First, that "the search for the good [is] a probabilistic activity, one that is always tied to a specific situation."[8] The second conviction "concerns the dignity of peoples and hence the respect due to their customs and cultures understood as expressions of their particular ways of life."[9] The good or true must be filtered through the consciousness of individuals, and the family is our first teacher in the particular manners and mores of our nation. The family teaches us rudimentary, but powerfully relevant, lessons of justice, honor, piety, loyalty, and the less noble but paramount lessons of manners and etiquette that allow us to predict what others in our society will do and thus allow for societal cohesion without the coercive force of the state. Without these lessons of particularity cooperation would only occur by written rules backed by the force of the state. All these lessons in how to behave reflect elements of truth and the good; they all point outside the particular to some kind of universality, but it is only later, when our reason has matured that we are able to look outward at the universal goods that these manners and mores represent. No matter what, though, our recognition of what is good and true is always filtered through the particularity that we learned at our parents' knees.

The lessons of the particular and its relationship to the universal that the family teaches do not end with lessons of goodness or truth. In an important sense, the particularity of the family points to universal truths about the human condition, but it does so in a way that makes these truths bearable. Through the experience of particular tragedies we become gradually accustomed to the insufficiency and imperfection of human life. The family exposes us to the tragic elements of life while insulating us from the full force of human tragedy. Childhood tragedies like moving to a new neighborhood, losing a pet (or worse, a relative), teach us lessons about the world. Our families help determine how we deal with these losses while assuring us that we are still anchored to this particular life, not left to drift aimlessly, even in the face of extreme grief.

Over time these human tragedies become more profound. Pets are replaced by grandparents, and eventually, parents. Sometimes we lose children. But throughout all of these tragedies we have supporting characters filling roles of support and attachment, and we are tied to these characters whether we like it or not. The metaphor of the family as anchor is particularly apt here, since the family prevents us from being carried away by grief. If the tragedy involves a family member, we have other relations who are bound to us in that same grief. If the tragedy involves something external to the family, we are anchored by the love and affection of our relations who at the same time provide us with duties and responsibilities that must be fulfilled even in the face of anguish. Children, elderly relatives, and spouses create obligations of care that persist and allow us to gradually return to life by forcing us to participate in small daily acts of living.

THE BREAKDOWN OF THE FAMILY

Despite the centrality of the family in human life, it is not as hardy as one might assume. The family as an institution is fragile and can be broken down by any of a combination of social, political, legal, and economic pressures. Delsol's discussion of subsidiarity is particularly important here.[10] Delsol's distinction between roles and functions provides a useful tool for understanding how familial roles are co-opted and turned into functions by the state. More importantly, this distinction serves to demonstrate how the power of the family is inversely proportional to the power of the state.

Before we discuss the breakdown of the family it makes sense to discuss precisely how the family serves as a counterbalance to the state. In the first place, the family restricts the kinds of laws that can be passed. Parents resent and resist legislation that determines how they raise their children. The contention surrounding the right to reproductive freedom attests to the primal importance of reproduction and family concerns in human life. Policies like China's One-Child Policy provoke rioting even among a people accustomed to oppressive governmental force. The family is in some ways the base line for acceptable laws, creating a basic private sphere in which small groups operate largely free from state coercion. The family is the home to freedom of conscience and speech in their most basic form. Our law recognizes the private family sphere by preserving spousal privilege (and usually parent-child privilege by extension), which preserves the sanctity of familial relationships from interference by the state, even when paramount state interests are at stake.

The family restricts the power of the state by fulfilling the roles that, in the hands of the state, become functions. As Delsol points out, when the family falls apart or diminishes in importance, people slip through the cracks. Part of this is the result of what Delsol describes as the shift from care-giving to productivity. In an effort to open up society's productive functions to women, we have shifted the focus away from care-giving. In so doing, we allow women an unprecedented place in the modern world, but this new-found freedom comes at a cost: "The contempt for care-giving activities has at length left out in the cold more and more individuals who cannot be traded for merchandise . . . but who remain deprived of vigilant care, including delinquent children, the lonely elderly, and so on down the list of all the socially disinherited."[11] When the family is weak, there is nothing left to do but replace familial roles with the functions of caretakers. Hospitals, halfway "houses," foster "homes," and nursing "homes" all attempt to mimic the care of family without the emotional attachment. People's physical needs are met while their psychological and mental needs increase. Recent reports on the high rate of suicide and crime among the elderly in Japan is indicative of a society where the family has lost its impact, and where individuals are set adrift to survive or not.[12] Without the family, individual flourishing is impossible, and the result is an increase in social ills like crime, suicide, and a lack of what is now called social capital.

The family restricts the power of the state in one more important theoretical sense, in that the family reminds us that imperfection is part and parcel of the human experience, and that legislation, lawsuits, and regulations cannot prevent tragedy and loss. The family serves as the final and stalwart barrier to the pursuit of perfection and the modern technological mission to turn all human tragedy into problems to be solved (a shift Delsol describes as turning "troubles" into "problems").[13] Because of its moderate position between the individual and the community the family is the moderating force that prevents either liberalism or egalitarian democracy from falling into dangerous excess. The most radical kinds of utopias are usually stymied by the family before they become dangerous to individuals. The Israeli kibbutzim were forced to moderate their position on radical egalitarianism because mothers persisted in the recognition that motherhood is the role of an individual, not the function of the community.[14]

The family is not impervious to cultural changes, however. As the respect for traditional norms and values diminishes, the status of the family decreases. A decreased respect for the family opens the door for new, less stable familial structures (like the single-mother household) which create a new set of political consequences. The family in its diminished form is incapable of fulfilling the roles of parent and child. Increasingly, the state is asked to step into the breach. Family roles gradually become state functions, and as family roles become state functions, the state gains power over individual lives. The increasing precedence of foster care and family court, required by the breakdown of the family, puts immense power into the hands of unelected social workers and judges. The need to provide security in old age and support the impoverished and those with mental illness supports the growth of massive government bureaucracies and legitimates increasingly large tax burdens.

The political system is thus in a state of tension with the family. The power relationship between the two is an inverse one, and each benefits when the other decays. But leaving aside the postmodern focus on power relations, the relationship can be seen are more symbiotic. The family provides the state with much needed stability, creating law-abiding citizens who have been trained in the basic norms and values of the culture. There is thus an uneasy agreement among most moderate political groups that the family should be supported, but the rationale for the importance of the family is unclear, usually based on a kind of emotional attachment rather than a rational belief that the family fills a necessary role.

The most danger to the family comes from the extremes of the political spectrum—the groups that desire either radical liberty or radical equality. These groups see the family as an unwanted source of stability—the very thing that prevents the institutional change that allows for progress. Political traditions based on freedom often depict the family as a social construct that merely camouflages the radical liberty of the individual. Libertarian philosophers' work on the family is usually characterized by mere neglect. Neglect is never completely benign, however, since a radical focus on freedom and consent undermines the hierarchical structure of the family that gives it its strength. For radical libertarians, a family is anything that people consent to, and can include a wide variety of more or less stable family forms. There is then nothing inherently negative about a single-parent household, despite the often negative effects on children and the corresponding increase in the power of the state that single parent households support (a side effect one would expect libertarians to want to avoid). However, the libertarian neglect of the family is probably less damaging to the family than those political orientations based on progressive equality. Liberal progressivism, based on a changing human nature, sees human institutions as capable of radical flux, and the family is no less immune to this flux than other institutions. If laws and governments are simply the will of the majority, it seems reasonable to assume that the family is infinitely changeable as well. The goal of progressives is, of course, a generally benevolent one. If the family is the root of inequality (and therefore of injustice) it seems in accord with (or even required by) justice to eradicate the hierarchical family and its

unequal outputs to create a society based on cooperative relationships between equal individuals who are given the same opportu-
nities to flourish.

The liberal tendency, whatever its protestations to the contrary,
is to see the family as the fundamental challenge to the liberal
democratic principles of democracy, consent, and equal opportunity. The egalitarian focus of progressive liberals forces us to lose
sight of the commonsense truth that human goods do not always
support each other. Consent, democracy, and equal opportunity are
all valuable goods, as are equality and liberty. But these values
mean nothing as universals until they have been applied to the
particulars of human life and filtered through the peculiar imperfec-
tions of human nature. Human existence precludes the perfect ful-
fillment of any value, and thus requires compromise and tolerance
for imperfect social arrangements. It is not necessarily then the
progressive liberal support for equality that is problematic for the
family, but the progressive intolerance for imperfection. This intolerance for imperfection and our impatience of suffering Delsol believes forces us away from the particular solace that the family
offers into an obsessive and ultimately unsuccessful search for universal solutions. [15]

The political problem posed by the family is ultimately the problem of imperfection. The family, rooted solidly in the moderate
stage between the particular and the universal, represents the tragedy of the human condition at the same time that it represents its
peculiar richness. Equality and liberty are not possible in their most
extreme forms because the family creates inequality at the same
time that it robs us of the basic freedoms to choose the lives we
want and the kinds of states in which we live. The family makes
political utopianism of every stripe illusory and incapable of real-
ization. The belief that we are individuals and free from the shackles of our birth is an illusion, as anyone who has struggled to cut or
loosen the bonds of family, but to no effect, can testify.

At the same time, the family is home to the most foundational and deepest attachments humanity is capable of. The love of parent for child, siblings for each other, and grandparents for their lineage is a profound emotion that links past, present and future. These emotional attachments fulfill deep human longings and make life meaningful and worth living. Those who are tragically born without families struggle to find their place in the world, navigating the treacherous path of non-consanguineous human relationships, and very often attempt to create a new family in the void by marrying and having children of their own. Moreover, the very tragedies that family life creates, whether the loss of loved ones or our bondage to imperfect people, are precisely the kinds of situations that create what used to be known as character. Tragedy can reveal "men's capabilities and character."[16] More importantly, "the tragic is the bearer of meaning."[17]

The family is thus an example, cause, and solution to the imperfection in human life. Or, as Delsol puts it, the family is an answer to man's insufficiency.[18] Humans are forced into tradeoffs, compromises, and imperfect agreements, forced to recognize the limitations posed by other humans, internal conflicts and external pressures. The family reminds us that we are limited and restricted, but it makes amends for those restrictions by providing us with a place in the world and a sense of belonging.

Moderate philosophers like Delsol, who wrote of Montesquieu what could apply to herself, that he "hewed to a narrow and complex path between relativism and dogmatism,"[19] recognize the imperfection inherent in human life while also paying respect to the human desire for the universal or the good. In order for politics to recognize these tensions in human life, it must learn to walk the complex path between the individual and community, between particularity and universality, between imperfection and perfection.

Part of this politically moderate project involves recognizing the moderating influence of the family and its importance as a foundational aspect of human flourishing.

Delsol reminds us that "totalitarianism, of whatever persuasion, emerges when we get caught up in the belief that 'everything is possible.'"[20] The family reminds us continually that not everything is possible, but it provides us ample solace in our suffering.

NOTES

1. Chantal Delsol, *The Unlearned Lessons of the Twentieth Century: An Essay on Late Modernity*, trans. Robin Dick (Wilmington, DE: ISI Books, 2006).

2. Adam Smith, *The Theory of Moral Sentiments* (Indianapolis: Liberty Fund, 1982) 219, 313.

3. Edmund Burke, *Reflections on the Revolution in France*, *Select Works of Edmund Burke, Vol. II*, ed. Francis Canavan (Indianapolis, IN: Liberty Fund), 136.

4. *Unlearned Lessons*, 140.

5. Chantal Delsol, *Icarus Fallen: The Search For Meaning in an Uncertain World*, trans. Robin Dick (Wilmington, DE: ISI Books, 2003), 139.

6. *Theory of Moral Sentiments*, 219.

7. Ibid., 235.

8. Chantal Delsol, *Unjust Justice: Against the Tyranny of International Law*, trans. Robin Dick (Wilmington, DE: ISI Books, 2008), 32.

9. *Unjust Justice*, 33.

10. While much of that work is in French (including her book *The Subsidiary State*), one can get gleanings of her argument, especially in terms of how it relates to the family, throughout the works available in English.

11. *Icarus Fallen*, 156.

12. http://www.telegraph.co.uk/news/worldnews/asia/japan/3213349/Japan-struggles-with-elderly-crime-wave.html.

13. *Icarus Fallen*, 203.

14. Lionel Tiger, *Women in the Kibbutz* (New York: Harcourt Brace Jovanovich, 1975).

15. *Icarus Fallen*, 205.

16. *Icarus Fallen*, 210.

17. *Icarus Fallen*, 241.

18. *Unlearned Lessons*, 58.

19. *Unjust Justice*, 32.

20. Ibid., 11.

Index

About the Editors

Lauren K. Hall is assistant professor of political science at the Rochester Institute of Technology. She has published numerous articles on issues in modernity, including biotechnology, the emotions, and the family. She is currently working on a book on the political role of the family, which expands on the essay in this volume.

Paul Seaton is associate professor of philosophy at St. Mary's Seminary and University in Baltimore, Maryland. He is the translator of several books by French authors, including Chantal Delsol, Pierre Manent, and Rémi Brague. He has published widely on ancient, modern, and contemporary political philosophy.

CPSIA information can be obtained at www.ICGtesting.com
Printed in the USA
BVOW072343151211

278297BV00003B/4/P